THE POWERSHIFT PRINCIPLE

Empowering Yourself through

Life's Challenges

by
Tamara Vaughn J.D. LL.M

success NRG inc.

Punta Gorda, Florida

SuccessNRG, Inc.
1133 Bal Harbor Blvd
Suite 1139 PMB 125
Punta Gorda, Florida 33950
www.SuccessNRG.com

The stories of the author's clients profiled in this book have been published with
their permission. No attorney-client privilege has been violated. Out of respect for
their privacy, however, the author has changed their names.

Scripture quotations marked NKJV are taken from the New King James Version.
Copyright© 1979, 1980, 1982 by Thomas Nelson, Inc.

Scripture quotations marked (NIV) are taken from the HOLY BIBLE, NEW
INTERNATIONAL VERSION®. NIV®. Copyright© 1973, 1978, 1984 by International Bible Society. Used by permission of Zondervan. All rights reserved.

Scripture quotations marked (NLT) are taken from the Holy Bible, New Living
Translation, Copyright©1996. Used by permission of Tyndale House Publishers,
Inc. Wheaton, Illinois 60189. All rights reserved.

Scripture quotations taken from the Amplified® Bible, Copyright © 1954, 1958,
1962, 1964, 1965, 1987 by The Lockman Foundation. Used by permission.
(www.Lockman.org)

Author photographs Katie Meehan © 2008
Cover Design by Jonathan Guinn, Guinn Design

Library of Congress Cataloging-in-Publication Data

Publisher's Cataloging-in-Publication (Provided by Quality Books, Inc.)

Vaughn, Tamara.
   The powershift principle : empowering yourself through life's challenges / Tamara Vaughn.
      p.   cm.
   LCCN 2008905505
   ISBN-13: 978-0-9818505-0-4
   ISBN-10: 0-9818505-0-2

1. Success--Psychological aspects. 2. Suffering.
3. Self-actualization (Psychology)   I. Title. II. Title:
Power shift principle.

BF637.S8V38 2008   158.1
                   QBI08-600178

Printed in the United States of America August 2008

This book is dedicated to:

My father, Arthur R. Vaughn, whose disabilities
strengthened my abilities,

And to my mother, Betty R. Vaughn

My grandmother, Lucille Beasley

And my aunt, Alligene Sanders

The women in my life whose strength, courage, determination
and love shaped my values and beliefs.

ACKNOWLEDGMENTS

I want to express my Gratitude to the PowerShift Partners who
have supported and encouraged me during this project:

Thank you to my mother, Betty Vaughn. She has always given
me her love and support in all my endeavors. Her belief in me
allowed me to manifest this dream, master this goal and step
onto my path of purpose. Mom, I love you!

Thank you to my friend, Diana Donlon, a true PowerShift
Partner. She was my cheering section, fan club and editor as
I wrote and re-wrote each chapter. She continued to hold the
vision of this book and its journey. Thank you for being my
friend and my guide on the path to publication.

And to God, my ultimate PowerShift Partner. The book that
you are holding is not the book that I first began to write.
This is His book and the glory belongs to Him.

THE POWERSHIFT PRINCIPLE

Table of Contents

CHAPTER
ONE

POWER STRUGGLES

"If adversity moves us to rediscover ourselves and the God within us, it becomes an important ally. Pain and challenge are the Universe's way of getting our attention so we can shift direction from loss to success."
— *Alan Cohen*

The nurse looked at me in amazement. "If I had been through what you had been through they would have to put me in a straight jacket!"

I sat anxiously in the doctor's office giving a detailed explanation of the challenging events that had taken place in my life during the previous year. Would this seemingly detached regurgitation of facts offset any negative medical findings from my check-up? Would it negate the effects of the physical and mental stress I had experienced? Throughout the drama that had encompassed the preceding months, I had managed to maintain my composure. The recitation of my story to my doctor was an attempt to validate my exhaustion and find some rationalization for the challenges I had endured.

Leaving the office with a clean bill of health, I thought, "Yes, I have been through a lot."

In the preceding 14 months, I had married for the first time. I was 42. My husband and I moved into my house when we returned home from our honeymoon. Eight days later, we were hit by Hurricane Charley, a category four storm. The roof of the house was severely damaged. We were dealt an additional blow within weeks as the outer bands of Hurricanes Frances and Jeanne wreaked further havoc on the area. The integrity of the roof was already compromised and could not withstand the additional stress of the winds and rains. The ceilings crashed to the floors exposing broken trusses and leaving soaking wet piles of insulation and drywall in each room. Like many in the area, the house and its contents were almost a total loss.

My husband and I moved into a motor home parked in the driveway. My parents shared the same property with me. My mother and father were relegated to three rooms in the house that were still somewhat inhabitable.

Several months later, I had to euthanize one of my horses. Although his heart and spirit never surrendered, River had been chronically ill for several years and the strain of his illness had finally overcome his body's abilities. As the one-year anniversary of Hurricane Charley approached, my mother had a stroke. My father was also diagnosed with cancer of the esophagus and an inoperable abdominal aneurysm.

At this point, a little more than a year had passed since Hurricane Charley had interrupted my life in August 2004. The house was nowhere close to being completed. I fired the contractor, who happened to be my husband. We divorced shortly thereafter. I spent the next year coordinating the rebuilding of the house and, as I had done before, managing to rebuild my life.

These challenges were not minor daily inconveniences and difficulties. These ordeals were major life adversities. They were also not the first run of significant events to present me with such challenges.

At 17, during the last semester of my senior year in high school, I became afflicted with anorexia. I entered college and continued struggling with the disease. Until the age of 22 my life was focused on food - or the lack thereof - diet pills, laxatives and exercising my 5- foot, 7- inch frame down to 85 pounds.

Just as I recovered from this debilitating disorder, my father suffered an injury to his brain. A sinus infection had become severe and worked its way into the brain cavity causing effects similar to a stroke. My father was mentally and physically disabled at age 52 and was never able to work again. In my junior year of college at the age of 23, I had to leave my education for a later date to become a caretaker and provider for my father, along with my mother.

My father's illness placed us in serious financial distress. Debt was high and there were extremely difficult months. My mother and I struggled to make ends meet. We worked full time and coped with the daily challenges of caring for a mentally and physically disabled person.

Eventually, however, the turmoil diminished. Finances began to improve and life returned to a daily routine. At that time, I chose to finish my education and continue on to law school. I graduated with my Juris Doctorate and decided to specialize in Estate Planning. Pursuing my Master of Laws degree added another year to my studies.

Three months out of school, I was scheduled to open my office on August 24, 1992. As fate would have it, the area in which I lived, Homestead, Florida, took a direct hit from Hurricane Andrew on that very day. This category five storm left my parents and me homeless, as it did to so many others. All of our material belongings were gone or totally destroyed.

In many ways, all the events that transpired subsequent to Hurricane Charley appeared to be a repeat performance. In moments where I actually had the time to think about what was going on in my life, I contemplated the number and severity of the challenges that I had experienced. Had I signed some unknown karmic contract? Was I atoning for actions in a past life? Could all of this be just some fortuitous roll of the dice? Or, had I done something to irritate or disappoint God? The answers to my questions became clearer as I navigated each challenge.

"...And God is faithful. He will not allow the test to be more than you can stand. When you are tested, He will show you a way out so that you can endure."
— *1 Corinthians 10:13 (NLT)*

Trials and tribulations, challenges and changes: the catalysts for true transformation in our lives. Let's face it, when things are comfortable we do not like to mix it up. Most of us do not intentionally provoke problems and pressures in our lives. However, when we are confronted with stress and discomfort, adversity can provide one of our most important growth experiences.

The character of our souls can be defined in the very moments when we have the opportunity to create inner peace within the midst of the external circumstances that represent the source of our pain. Our intuitive awareness can be raised in the solitary silence where we feel wholly isolated and alone. Creativity can be generated to stimulate the possibility of new ideas and innovative methods to solve or transcend the situation. Our relationship with God can be strengthened so that the Light of His Love will shine on us in what we believe to be our darkest hour. Adversities can present us with the most dynamic, resourceful, inspirational and productive moments in our lives.

In the midst of our challenges, however, we many times engage in a pre-programmed download of emotions and reactions based on past experiences or a perceived reality. We often create further turmoil and emerge from the confusion and chaos beaten, battered and exhausted. We may rationalize some sense of victory and accomplishment to validate our wounds and scars. The goal and primary focus become survival as we may choose only to react to the circumstances and situations with which we are confronted. We often become so embedded in the momentary madness that we fail to plan a course of action to manage or direct the events that are affecting our lives. This type of behavior perpetuates a cycle of what I call situational insanity. Our confidence and feelings of self-worth may become further diminished. It is only natural to experience fear and self-doubt when faced with what may seem an insurmountable challenge. However, once these two critics merge with stress and exhaustion, the remnants of self-esteem can quickly turn to self-pity.

Transformation occurs when we come to a crossroad where we are truly tired of experiencing the pain and we have expended what we believe is our last ounce of stamina from our mental, physical and emotional body. We search within our spiritual self to find the inner resilience and fortitude to shift from a point of self-preservation to a position of self-empowerment. It is when our spiritual energy is ignited in the midst of adversity that we come face to face with our inner greatness. In that moment, there is a *PowerShift*.

"But those who trust in the Lord will find new strength. They will soar high on wings like eagles. They will run and not grow weary. They will walk and not faint."
— *Isaiah 40:31 (NLT)*

How do you get through the challenges in your life? How do you go from survive to thrive? Winston Churchill said, "If you're going through hell, keep going." You do not always make good major life decisions in the middle of major life adversities. You cannot resolve a challenge with the same energy and thought process that contributed to or created that challenge in the first place. I have first-hand experience that to both survive and thrive in the midst of life altering challenges, *the PowerShift Principle* becomes a necessary resource to steady the course of the transition.

The PowerShift Principle is a source of energy that allows you to turn off all the external noise, situations and circumstances and go within your soul and spirit to find inner peace. This is the place where you discover your point of true power. Your inner resources are where your greatness is first manifested. Your inner guidance is your source of information and inspiration. A *PowerShift* is simply a change in the influences that control your being. In shifting the power from the external chaos and confusion to the inner focus, you are able to reclaim the self to the state that is connected with God. The inner peace and power is the origin of your wisdom, strength, motivation and creativity. From this point, you can transcend adversity, master goals and manifest dreams.

There are eight primary tools or *PowerShifts* that create *the PowerShift Principle*. Each one stands independently of the others. Utilized together, however, their strength and effectiveness intensifies. These tools enable you to empower and nurture yourself spiritually, physically, mentally and emotionally.

POWERSHIFT #1: Purpose

The first *PowerShift* of *the PowerShift Principle* is Purpose. Purpose is the knowing or discovering of what it is that you are on this physical planet to do through emotional, moral and spiritual growth. It is your service to God, to yourself and to others. Some people immediately know their Purpose. For others, there is a gradual realization. Challenges offer the ability to strengthen your own inner resources, realize your gifts and talents and come into alignment with your Purpose. Adversity can take you beyond the realms of physical successes to unprecedented levels of significance. Challenges and adversity are the fast track to knowledge and experience to live a life in Purpose.

POWERSHIFT #2: Prayer

The second *PowerShift* of *the PowerShift Principle* is Prayer. Prayer is our level of communication with God. For some people, the only time that they pray is when they are faced with life's challenges. Prayer is seeking out God as you know Him and as you may come to know Him. In the midst of adversity, you may ask for guidance, relief or both. When I was younger, I thought God used challenges to get me down on my knees. There was a time when I mistakenly thought that tough times were a result of me not being good enough or for punishment of some wrong that I had committed. As I have grown in my relationship with God, I stay on my knees, in a figurative sense, to embrace His love and the strength that I derive from my relationship with Him. When I look back at my greatest challenges, it was His power that sustained me, even when I failed to ask.

POWERSHIFT #3: Divine Direction

The third *PowerShift* of *the PowerShift Principle* is Divine Direction. After you invoke the Divine Presence into your life through Prayer, you must remain open to receiving the messages. Divine Direction is the level at which God communicates with you. This tool encompasses the signs, the intuitions, the dreams and the people that are directed into your life to act as guideposts in the midst of challenges and adversities. They may provide the answers to your prayers, the direction to take to transform or transcend the adversity in your life, or the lessons within the challenge providing you with the opportunity for growth.

POWERSHIFT #4: Time and Focus

The fourth *PowerShift* of *the PowerShift Principle* is Time and Focus. Focus is how, where and on what you expend your Time and energy. You can easily waste these valuable resources when a challenge arises. It is the ability to appropriately determine the proper expenditure of your time and energy so as not to cause exhaustion through the exertion of effort on needless and unnecessary tasks.

POWERSHIFT #5: Words and Thoughts

The fifth *PowerShift* of *the PowerShift Principle* is Words and Thoughts. The power to transcend or transform any adversity is within the control of your mind. This control is dependent on your ability to take power over the Words that you say and the Thoughts that you think. In the face of life's challenges, you must be able to counteract the negative external influences that may attempt to penetrate your mind. Your Thoughts and Words must be positive and constructive, rather than negative and destructive.

POWERSHIFT #6: PowerShift Partners

The sixth *PowerShift* of *the PowerShift Principle* is *PowerShift* Partners. In the midst of life's challenges, it is imperative to connect with and cultivate a strong and supportive network of people who will offer encouragement and motivation. Partners are the people who see your strengths, talents and gifts when you do not. They may suggest new directions and offer new possibilities when you have found yourself off focus. Partners offer you emotional, mental and spiritual preservation.

POWERSHIFT #7: Forgiveness

The seventh *PowerShift* of *the PowerShift Principle* is Forgiveness. Forgiveness allows you to transcend any adversity or transform any challenge into a positive situation. When you Forgive, you are willing to make a conscious choice to release the baggage that you have accumulated. This baggage is composed of all of the hurt feelings, fears, resentments, disappointments and unanswered expectations. The negative energies created by the failure to Forgive may create a stronghold within the adversity. True progress in extricating yourself from the challenge may be delayed as a result of your desire to hold onto the past. Forgiveness is the *PowerShift* that allows you to concentrate on your future.

EIGHT POWERSHIFT PRINCIPLES

- **Purpose**
- **Prayer**
- **Divine Direction**
- **Time and Focus**
- **Words and Thoughts**
- **Partners**
- **Forgiveness**
- **Gratitude**

POWERSHIFT #8: *Gratitude*

The eighth *PowerShift* of *the PowerShift Principle* is Gratitude. Gratitude is the ability to be thankful even during the tough times. It shifts your focus and allows you to concentrate on the positive events despite the challenges or transitions that you may be experiencing in your life. Being thankful for your abilities and blessings minimizes the stress and discomfort while dealing with that which is difficult and demanding.

Together, these eight tools comprise *the PowerShift Principle*. They are of critical importance during challenges, adversities and transitions and they are vital to your life force on a day to day basis. The *PowerShifts* are your protective gear to insulate you from the outside events and external chaos. They are your weapons to combat the negative energies that are the by-product of any challenge or adversity. The *PowerShifts* are also the keys to mastering your goals and manifesting your dreams.

*"For God has not given us a spirit of fear and timidity,
but of power, love and self- discipline."*
— *2 Timothy 1:7(NLT)*

We are confronted with a multitude of challenges and conflicts on a daily basis. Some are minor and seemingly insignificant in the course of our lives. Others are greater and more intense, involving life-altering experiences. There are those that are the result of some negative event. Others are challenges created through some positive experience that stretch us beyond present abilities. Whatever the origin of the challenge, adversity is an education with highly individualized lessons.

I developed *the PowerShift Principle* in my life to manage challenges, adversities and transitions, and to achieve my goals and live my dreams. I continue to improve my skills and to take advantage of the lessons that I learn during times of stress and discomfort. When I put the *PowerShifts* into practice, I can move beyond my present abilities and go through or transcend the adversity. When I stop the external struggle and call on my inner resources, challenges become less dramatic and transitions become less traumatic. The *PowerShifts* allow me to position myself for greater things that are to manifest subsequent to the challenge or transition.

I have been told on several occasions that God doesn't give you more than you can handle. Quite frankly, at times I think that He has overestimated my present abilities. Mother Teresa expressed a similar sentiment when she said, "I know that God will not give me anything I can't handle. I just wish that He didn't trust me so much."

One of the single greatest challenges of my life was overcoming an eating disorder that consumed my entire being for five years. It was during this time that *the PowerShift Principle* first originated. I became anorexic at the age of 17, during the second semester of my senior year in high school.

Anorexia is an eating disorder that is characterized by a refusal to maintain the minimal normal body weight. It is a serious and often chronic, life-threatening mental illness. The key characteristics of this disorder include an intense fear of gaining weight and a distorted body image. The severe, restrictive caloric consumption and subsequent weight loss can cause starvation and other related medical complications. Some of the physical consequences are so serious as to result in death.

I began to diet, as do many teenage girls, to lose five pounds before purchasing my prom dress. Adolescent girls and young women are particularly vulnerable to anorexia because they have a tendency to go on strict diets in an effort to achieve the ideal body. My diet was successful and I accomplished my initial goal before prom. The diet didn't stop there, however, and I continued to lose weight. For the person with anorexia, there is a satisfaction in the control which is achieved over weight and food. This control becomes the focal point of his or her existence.

My senior year was active and demanding and my prospects for college were excellent. As is common for those afflicted with the disorder, I continuously strived for excellence in my academic studies. I was an honor student and a member of the gifted program. I was also drum major of my high school marching band and played an active role in the unit's successes at competition.

Outside the scholastic environment, I was competing in equestrian competitions. I was training my Thoroughbred and Quarter Horse in dressage and riding my Paso Fino mare in state and national shows. I began modeling as well. I participated on the runway in fashion shows and in front of the camera for print ads. During this time, I also experienced the pressures of applying to colleges and making the major life decisions expected of a high school senior.

The pain that I experienced and expressed through my eating disorder was a result of my incessant need to be perfect. Anything less to me was an embarrassment. Additional emotional conflict developed when the guidance counselors at my high school pressured me to send out scores of college applications. Their desire to help me succeed was overshadowed by their need to have another successful statistic for a college admission. I wanted to stay home and attend a community college for the first year or two. This would allow me to remain close to my horses and continue showing. The junior college environment would also offer me the opportunity to decide on a major in order to apply to the right school for my chosen field. The administration of my high school let me know that this choice wasn't good enough in light of my scholastic accomplishments.

Against their guidance, I made the decision to attend the local junior college. Despite the soundness of my reasoning, watching my peers leave for their respective universities at the end of the summer reinforced in my mind that I was failing to live up to my abilities and, therefore, failing.

I cannot pinpoint the moment that a simple diet turned deadly. However, until the age of 22, I plunged deeper into the abyss of this dietary hell with each passing day. The eating disorder established a stronghold in my mind and body and revealed a dark side of control, discipline and determination. The behaviors in which I engaged, mentally and physically consumed my time, energy and my life force itself.

Anorexics usually lose weight by reducing their total food intake and exercising excessively. The avoidance of fattening and high-calorie food combined with the exercise may cause an anorexic to appear merely health-conscious at first. My initial caloric restriction was gradual and I made healthy food choices for my meals. As the disorder progressed, however, my caloric consumption developed into severe deprivation. I consumed less than 250 calories per day. My main or only meal would consist of a properly portioned bowl of cream of wheat with fried egg whites. On the occasions that I had to eat in a restaurant, I would order a salad with vinegar and a dry baked potato. If the potato was accidentally served with butter or the salad came with dressing, I would experience a total break down and anxiety attack.

Despite the lack of sustenance and fuel for my body, I also obsessively exercised to the point of physical exhaustion. I had always disliked physical education classes in school because I was not athletically inclined. However, in my attempts to maintain control and lose more weight, I was running, swimming laps, doing calisthenics and engaging in any other exercise that would neutralize my caloric intake.

In my mind, the diet and exercise were not sufficient to fully utilize all the food that I had eaten. I began abusing laxatives and diuretics to purge my body of excess food and water. The term anorexia literally means loss of appetite. Anorexics do not lose their appetite. Instead they become disciplined enough to ignore it, or they find other ways to control the pangs of hunger and the desire to eat. I consumed diet pills and drank caffeinated diet drinks to stave off any feelings of hunger and to artificially charge my exhausted body with energy. Many anorexics sublimate their desire to eat by cooking for others. I cooked excessively and gave all of the food away to friends and neighbors.

During this time I was also attending college. I transferred from the community college in South Florida, where I began my collegiate education, to another junior college in central Florida. Fighting my feelings of failing, I applied to and was accepted by a private university to major in business. In an effort to find a place where I felt I belonged, I transferred from there to another school, declaring a new major after only one semester. This process continued several more times. Having no true direction, I was choosing majors and schools to please and prove myself to other people.

Anorexia is a testament to the power of the mind. My mind had a destructive, obsessive control over my body and my weight plummeted from 135 pounds to 87 pounds on a 5'7" frame. My face became hollow, dark circles appeared under my eyes and bones protruded. One of the most terrifying aspects of the disorder is that people with anorexia continue to believe that they look fat despite their skeleton-like appearance. As with many anorexics, my hair thinned and my nails became brittle. I bruised easily and was always cold. Depression is common in people suffering from this disorder and I felt like a dark cloud hung over my life.

The dichotomy of this disease is that I was out of control trying to maintain control. The lifestyle and focus of an anorexic is difficult to sustain. The dominating discipline creates a harsh, restrictive daily regimen. My full focus was on food or the lack thereof. My mind was consumed with thoughts of how to avoid eating and, if I had to eat, how to rid myself quickly of the caloric effects. If I could not purge myself of what food I ate without raising the suspicion of those around me, then I had to counteract the calories ingested. As I became more physically fatigued and mentally exhausted, the disorder gained strength. Each morning I awakened only to wonder why God did not take me the night before.

During this deadly downward spiral, I saw doctors, therapists and nutritionists. There was little known about the disorder during the early 1980's and there were few treatment options available. My mother took me for an interview at Shands, a hospital in Gainesville, Florida, that was known for the treatment of eating disorders. Being a people pleaser, I would assure each of the professionals attempting to help me that I was doing better and making improvement. After I left their respective offices, I would continue the same course of actions.

As an anorexic, if you are not one of those that overcome the disease, you can be condemned to practicing this disorder and engaging in this behavior throughout your life. You may find yourself living on the brink between life and death. There are also those that fully succumb to the disorder. The *PowerShift* that was the turning point during this adversity began as a result of an intervention of the Divine kind. I now refer to this moment as my spiritual kick in the butt.

> *"You may not realize it when it happens, but a kick in the teeth may be the best thing in the world for you."*
> — *Walt Disney*

The Divine Intervention came in the form of a dream. I have a deep love for animals and it is that God-given gift that I most cherish. In this dream, I was standing in front of a white fence overlooking a lush, green pasture. In the distance I saw my horses grazing peacefully. As I proceeded towards them, I was stopped by a Being that was present behind my left shoulder. Referring to the horses, the Being simply said, "They aren't yours anymore." These were the words that saved my life.

In the depths of my depression, my thought process had become so distorted and damaged that I thought that my friends and family would be fine if anything happened to me. My self-esteem was so diminished that I believed no one would miss me if I died. I was too busy holding on to my own feelings of unworthiness to accept the love of my parents and friends. That changed when I awoke from the dream.

"They aren't yours anymore" struck a deep maternal chord in my being. I had always been committed to the love and care of my animals, but I had never taken the time to think about what would happen to my horses if I were no longer able or present to care for them. God used my animals to save my life. He knew the one gift that He could use to reach deep in the recesses of my mind and find me again. He then gave me the strength to find myself. I suddenly had a strong need and desire to overcome and defeat this adversary that had consumed my life for five years.

The Divine Intervention was the catalyst for the shift. I cannot pinpoint the day the diet turned deadly, but I can pinpoint the moment that I had the opportunity to choose life or death. I chose life. The dream was my Message. I now had to put forth the effort and take responsibility to maintain the initial desire, determination and motivation. I had to initiate the necessary actions to support myself spiritually, mentally, emotionally and physically in the healing of my body and mind. During the months following this dream, the *PowerShifts* were put into place.

"A turning point is life's way of giving you a chance to move ahead spiritually, though you must reach for the gift yourself."
— *Harold Klemp*

First and foremost, I began a Prayer practice in order to spiritually support myself. In doing so, I relinquished the need for control that had driven me into the depths of my eating disorder and turned it over to God. Anorexics have a deep need for love. God's intervention was evidence of His love for me. I had been praying for God to take me. I now prayed that He would give me the strength to continue my recovery.

I also shifted the destructive Words and Thoughts that had previously taken authority over my mental and emotional processes. I spoke positive affirmations and filled my mind with constructive thoughts by reading self-help and spiritual books written by some of the greatest positive thinkers of our time. I listened to their audio books when I drove and also played them while I slept. Motivational and inspirational material constantly nourished my mind with its healing sustenance.

As the darkness lifted, the realization set in of just how long I had allowed the disorder to consume my life. I had affected my parents, my education, and my physical, mental and dental health. I had to release the guilt and shame and I had to let go of the anger. I had to Forgive myself and the disease that had taken five years of my life.

Forgiveness transformed into Gratitude. I was grateful for God's intervention. I was grateful for my health. Miraculously, the only lasting effect from the eating disorder was some damage to the enamel of my teeth. Anorexia has one of the highest mortality rates among the psychiatric disorders. Death can occur from medical complications or the severity of the depression can cause an anorexic to commit suicide. The strict caloric intake and the severe weight loss experienced by persons with anorexia can cause damage to the heart, the brain and to other vital organs. The body literally starts to feed off of itself for survival. The pulse rate can drop and the blood pressure can become extremely low. Anorexics may experience irregular heart rhythms or heart failure. The deprivation of food and lack of adequate and proper nutrition can cause calcium to leech from the bones, making them brittle and prone to breaks. In the worst-case scenario, anorexics can literally starve themselves to their death. Realizing what could have been my fate, I was grateful to be alive.

As I returned to an appropriate body weight, I surrounded myself with people who were supportive of my recovery and the positive changes to my body. The transition back into a healthy lifestyle and body image was not without its obstacles and challenges, however. Anorexics feel a strong sense of security within the parameters of their control. They feel safe within their illness. Gaining weight, even during recovery, is viewed as a loss of that control. My Partners were healthy-minded individuals who were there during those moments when I became anxious or stressed over food. They reminded me of all the positive steps that I had taken and the progress that I had made in reclaiming my life. They offered their encouragement and gave me their love as I learned to love myself.

In order to fully manifest my recovery, I had to redirect and realign my Focus with new intentions about my health and my weight. Calorie counting and the numbers on a scale had become my obsession. My Focus had been directed on how to manage or totally avoid my next encounter with food. As I regained healthy emotions and mental processes, my Focus shifted to healthy eating habits. Food was no longer the enemy. My workouts also changed from a rigorous regimen to a more relaxed routine. The Focus shifted from punishing my body to healing and strengthening my body.

The question remained as to what Purpose this challenge served in my life. There is not much known as to the true cause or causes of anorexia. Much of the research performed and data collected remains inclusive. However, certain personality traits such as low self-esteem and the desire for perfection are common among those afflicted with the disorder. Many, as was I, tend to be good students and excel at their chosen endeavors.

In retrospect, anorexia forced me to face issues about myself that needed to be addressed. Weight loss and food deprivation became a badge of mastery and control. Focusing on my weight, the one thing in my life that I believed that I could control, allowed me to disregard the real issues within my being. I was a high achiever, people-pleaser and perfectionist when it came to my performance. And yet, I never felt good enough. There is nothing wrong with striving to do your best. However, as an anorexic, the striving became a deadly driving and determination at all costs to physical and mental health. The disorder forced me to address my low self-esteem. I had to learn to love myself and separate who I was from what I did.

Typically, about half of those affected with anorexia will make a full recovery. Some will experience weight gain followed by a relapse. Others continue to deteriorate, remaining chronically ill throughout their lives. Some die. Overcoming the eating disorder strengthened me and allowed me to align myself with my life's Purpose. I tuned into the inner resources of my being to regain control of my mind in order to recover from anorexia. I conquered this deadly disorder and I learned that I had the strength and the ability to face any challenge that presented itself. I *Shifted the Power*!

"For our present troubles are small and won't last very long. Yet they produce for us a glory that vastly outweighs them and will last forever."
— *2 Corinthians 4:17(NLT)*

My experiences have proven to me that what may have seemed the darkest hour of my life gave way to the greatest moments of enlightenment. The insight and wisdom that I found during periods of adversity, challenges and transitions were of immeasurable value for the next step on the pathway of my life. In order to receive the gifts, however, I had to make the decision to release the external struggles, call on my inner resources and surrender to God.

I have always said that when you get off of the carousel, the roller coaster is the only other ride in the park. Life is full of ups and downs, peaks and valleys, victories and adversities. That is just life. It is how we are able to manage our minor upsets and our life-changing challenges that determine the level of spiritual, mental and emotional growth we experience. It is how we manage the challenges that will position us for the greatness to manifest in our lives.

The PowerShift Principle is not only a tool for self-empowerment during those times in life where there is stress and discomfort; it is a strategy for self-empowerment every day. Through the practice of the *PowerShifts*, there is an inner process of mental and spiritual maturity that develops and encourages your true inner power to emanate despite the external circumstances in which you may find yourself. *The PowerShift Principle* reinforces your faith in the power of God and restores your faith in yourself.

The stories contained within these pages are mine. It is in the darkest moments that we have the opportunity to see the brightest lights. When the lights have shown through the shadows onto our path and purpose, I believe that is our responsibility to show someone else the way. That is the purpose of this book. You are entitled to live a life of impact rather than settling for a powerless existence. You deserve to position yourself to realize the greatness within you and live a purpose-filled life. I celebrate your significance. Join me in that celebration! Let's *Shift the Power!*

CHAPTER
TWO

POWERSURGE: TRIALS AND TRIBULATIONS

"The true measure of a man is not how he behaves in moments of comfort and convenience but how he stands at times of controversy and challenges."
— *Martin Luther King Jr.*

In the midst of any adversity or challenge there is an overwhelming desire to ask the question, "Why me?" We have an innate need to know the reason, the cosmic answer or some universal motive for the existence of challenging events. We may rhetorically ask this question of ourselves. We may ask it of God. We may pose it to therapists or even psychics in an attempt to satisfy our need to find a logical answer where none may exist.

When we are faced with any challenge or adversity we have no right to ask, "Why me?" unless we ask the same question for every moment of peace, joy and happiness that we experience, as well. We do not search for answers when we get a raise, bonus or promotion. We do not search for answers and ask, "Why me?" when we find the man or woman of our dreams. We do not search for answers when there is a momentary lull in the events of the day and we are basking in an inner peace.

"In every adversity there lies the seed of an equivalent advantage. In every defeat is a lesson showing you how to win the victory next time."
— *Robert Collier*

Keep in mind that adversity is a learning tool and the curriculum is designed to teach you about yourself. The lessons give you insight into your strengths and weaknesses. Challenges encourage you to clarify your beliefs, values and needs. Adversity calls on you to seek out untapped resources, gifts and talents. It is a coach that can motivate you to stretch beyond the person you are presently and encourage you to embrace a glimpse of the person you are to become. Adversity is a guide that can direct you to the path of your purpose and personal greatness.

Instead of asking, "Why?" more appropriate questions to consider would be, "How does this adversity or challenge serve me?" "What am I learning?" "What is this challenge showing me about myself?" "How can I use this challenge to serve others?"

This may not seem like the easiest way to process events that overwhelm you. However, reprioritizing your questions in this manner allows you to shift from an ineffective and powerless perspective to a position of empowerment. Empowered, you will be more capable of making positive, thought-filled decisions and taking appropriate action under the circumstances.

"We know what we are,
but know not what we may be."
— *William Shakespeare*

Some challenges and adversities are so devastating that it is difficult to conceive of these empowering questions for months or years. As I have previously mentioned, another of my life's challenge is surviving the aftermath of Hurricane Andrew. I believe that a life can be forever changed in one brief moment. Andrew is evidence of that belief.

Hurricane Andrew arrived in the southern region of Miami Dade County, Florida at 3:30 a.m. on August 24, 1992. The storm ripped through the area with a vengeance. Three hours later, a path of mass destruction was left in its wake. Andrew's peak top wind speed was not directly calculated due to the total destruction and failure of the measuring instruments. However, it was estimated that the sustained winds were in excess of 165 miles per hour, with gusts exceeding 200 miles per hour. There were hundreds of thousands of people left homeless and unemployed. Monetary damages of the category 5 hurricane were in excess of $25 billion dollars (more than $41 billion in 2007 dollars). The physical, mental and emotional toll on the population, however, could not be calculated.

People were stripped of basic resources and means of survival. There was no electricity and the infrastructure of the power and telephone companies was severely damaged. Rubble lay where grocery stores once stood. Streets were unrecognizable with all identifying markers and buildings destroyed. Looters roamed the streets amid blocks of devastation looking to rob a victim of their last possessions.

Government assistance finally arrived almost two weeks later. The area resembled a war zone. The military built a tent city to house people left homeless from the hurricane. Units patrolled the streets to regain some order and control in the perimeter they established. Military helicopters flew overhead at night policing the remains of homes and businesses. The chopper pilots shined their spotlights over the devastation revealing an area that looked like it had been repeatedly bombed rather than hit by the forces of nature.

My parents and I were among the statistics. Our house and every material possession we owned were destroyed. Looking at the property after the storm, we saw remnants and pieces of our home, pictures, year books, furniture and clothes scattered over the yard. During the weeks after Andrew, we stood in long lines for food and ice. It was summer in Florida and the high temperatures and sun were extremely exhausting. My mother and I slept in my truck for the first few weeks, fighting off mosquitoes, the heat and the rain. Having no way to care for my disabled father, we sent him to a safe haven on the west coast of Florida for a month. Our days were spent attempting to salvage the bits and pieces that had been left and clearing the rest of the debris. It took weeks to locate resources for assistance. The rebuilding process took months and months turned into years.

Trying to fill the most basic of needs was a daily challenge. I had few clothes. Friends from other areas sent me some of their personal clothing to wear. Strangers sent basic necessities such as toothpaste and toilet paper. There was no electricity on my street for over four and a half months. MREs, meals ready to eat, were distributed by the military. I took a shower at night with a shower bag designed for camping. I filled it with cold water in the morning and the warmth of the sun somewhat heated it during the day. My friends and neighbors took baths in community lakes.

Small gestures of kindness were life-savers. Things that were once taken for granted were now considered luxuries. Two months after Andrew, my mother's friend asked us to spend the night at her house. Her electricity had been turned on a few days before and she had hot food and cold drinks. For the first time in weeks, I stood in a hot shower, letting the water beat down on my tired and aching muscles. I slept in her son's old room. He had left behind his waterbed when he went to college. My body sank into the mattress and was gently cushioned by the heated water soothing every muscle and joint. Those feelings, smells and sensations are forever ingrained in my memory.

Five months after Andrew hit, my parents and I were finally permitted the use of a FEMA mobile home. We had stayed in North Dade County for a few weeks in a small rented house that my mother had located through her real estate connections. The drive to our property in South Dade took over an hour and half each way. Although the distance was only thirty miles, there was still debris and military checkpoints to navigate. My tires were filled with plugs from all of the flats caused by nails, screws and other sharp objects that remained on the roads.

The Federal Emergency Management Agency moved our new home onto our property and we continued the rebuilding process. My mother and I spent the next two years putting our lives and our house back together. Matters that were pressing and important on August 23rd were no longer the focal point of my life on the morning of August 24th , 1992. I developed a great appreciation for many things previously taken for granted, such as a cool drink of water or an extra loaf of bread left by a neighbor at the gate. Volunteers who showed up with hammers and nails were all graciously and gratefully accepted. In the midst of such a life-changing experience, my perspective on what truly mattered was challenged and forever changed.

In the early morning hours of that Monday in August, the winds screamed their tormenting howl through the rumbles of the many tornadoes. The surging ocean flooded the area. It was one of the region's darkest and most devastating moments. South Florida, today, however, is in many ways stronger because of Andrew. The storm prompted massive rebuilding under tougher building codes and more scrutinized inspections. Disaster response was reviewed and rewritten in efforts to avoid the same atrocities, delays and failures that prevented victims from receiving prompt assistance.

The psychological and financial scars will continue to be felt for many years by the people who suffered the effects of Hurricane Andrew. For over a year-and-a-half after the storm, I woke up at 3:30 a.m. every day. This was the exact time that Andrew came on shore and I heard the train-like sound of the tornadoes tear through my neighborhood. Perhaps it was a form of post-traumatic stress syndrome. Maybe it was a gentle reminder of the many blessings I experienced throughout the ordeal.

Was I tempted to ask, "Why me?" Absolutely and without question! I wanted to know "why me?" Hurricane Andrew was actually projected to come ashore much farther north than at the point where it made landfall. Was I asking empowering questions during the first few months? No, I was trying to survive. The initial reaction to a devastating event or adversity is that it is surreal. I woke up the following day hoping and praying that it had been a bad dream. Then I remembered that the nightmare was real. Emotions ranged moment to moment from stress, anxiety, depression, frustration, irritation and anger. The survival instincts kicked in and

I got down to the business of piecing back together what was left of my life. In the unknown of any challenge there is only one certainty... life will never be the same. And, neither will you.

My questions and my subsequent perspective on the storm did change through the months and years that followed, however. The shift in perception was necessary in order to allow the healing process to take place. "What did I learn?" At that time, Hurricane Andrew was the worst national disaster to affect the United States. I learned that I did have the faith, fortitude, drive and determination to survive. I clarified my values and defined what was important to me. My family and my animals were spared from injury or death. Everything else could be repaired or replaced. My faith, values and beliefs sustained me and gave me comfort throughout each day subsequent to the storm.

My belief in God was intensified with the knowledge that He had protected what truly mattered in my life. I had been practicing law on the west coast of Florida in June and July and returned home the first of August. While I was working in Fort Myers, I had taken my horses with me and boarded them at a private facility. They had to remain on the west coast after I left because no one was available to trailer them back to Miami-Dade County. On August 24th, I knew that a guiding hand had prevented the return of my horses, knowing that they would have been killed. Their barn in South Dade was hit by a tornado and only the pad and footers remained.

Prior to Hurricane Andrew, there was television, telephones, cell phones, fast food restaurants and grocery stores. After the storm, there were no such conveniences. Locating the basic needs of food, water, shelter and a few items of clothing were a challenge. I was able to obtain some sense of physical comfort with what I had by defining that which was truly important and necessary. When I was finally able to enjoy such things as a movie or a television program or running through a drive-through and getting a quick bite to eat, I appreciated the privilege of doing so that much more.

"Show me someone who has done something worthwhile, and I'll show you someone who has overcome adversity."
— *Lou Holtz*

In experiencing any adversity or challenge, whether it is a natural disaster, the death of a loved one, a divorce or an addiction, the survivors have a unique ability and special gift to assist those who are experiencing the same or similar ordeals.

The first people arriving on the scene after Hurricane Andrew were people that had been affected by Hurricane Hugo in South Carolina. These volunteers appeared willingly and without being asked. They gave their time and energy, and offered assistance and compassion, knowing first-hand the challenges that the victims of Andrew faced.

Twelve years later, I was living in Punta Gorda when Hurricane Charley loomed in the Gulf of Mexico, stalking the shores of Florida. As with Andrew, the hurricane was projected to hit farther north. Again, its path changed and moved into my city. My home was severely damaged and compromised by Charley. The winds and rains of the outer bands of the two hurricanes that followed several weeks later caused further damage to the structure and to all my personal belongings.

After the wrath of Hurricane Charley passed through the area, I walked outside to assess the damage. I thanked God for everyone's safety and reminded Him that we had a deal. Since my experience with Andrew, as other storms approached, I reiterated in my prayers that one national disaster per lifetime was sufficient. The response from my statement was quick. A voice very clearly replied from within, "But you will help them get through it."

Over the next few weeks, I spoke at churches and service organizations about my life after Andrew. Drawing from my own personal experiences, I offered people some insight on what to expect from their emotions throughout the aftermath of the storm. In the middle of chaos, I offered them hope that they, too, could make it through the process that lay ahead. "Honor your feelings and respect where you are each day emotionally," I told them. Months later, people told me that on their worst days after the storm they remembered me and my stories of Andrew. They knew that if I could survive and later thrive after Andrew, they could restore their life after Charley.

On many occasions I have also had the opportunity to speak to men and women who are recovering from addictive behaviors. Whether it be an eating disorder, alcoholism or a drug addiction, they appear to be guided into my path.

One day I was at a book store reviewing the titles in the self-help section. A gentleman came up to me and asked, "Do you know of a good meditation book?" I assisted him in his search. Later, he shared with me that he had just been released from a 30-day rehabilitation unit for drug addiction. "I am a veteran and I served my country overseas during war," he told me. "I asked my counselors how to stay clean. Their answers gave me no true direction or indication on how to win my battle with drugs."

On his own, he made the decision to try meditation. That decision brought our paths together in the book store. I shared with him the story of my recovery from anorexia, and he knew that I understood the road that was before him. Together, we found a book on meditation for beginners and a spiritual book on taking authority over your mind. We then went to the books-on-tape section where I helped him pick out some positive motivational CDs. Afterwards, he thanked me and we said good-bye. My job was done. My purpose, as he stepped into my path, was to offer compassion, empathy, encouragement and a little bit of what had worked for me. He and God would take it from there.

Physical structures can be repaired and rebuilt with drywall, shingles, hammers and nails. Material possessions can eventually be replaced. The lives that are affected by any devastating event, addiction or tragedy must be rebuilt with love, understanding and compassion. Those that have been through such a challenge have a unique perception and inner knowing of how best to assist others to make it through the same situation or circumstance. It is not just sympathy or an understanding. The knowledge is empathy and the true ability to share in the emotions and experiences. It is the power to say, "I made it through and so can you!"

"With every adversity is planted the seed of an equivalent or greater benefit."

— *Napoleon Hill*

When faced with adversity or challenges, the first and foremost goal is usually to attempt to reduce the pain and suffering. We want to return to a normal way of life and find the comfort zone once again. Although easing the level of discomfort is a worthwhile endeavor, it can not become the only objective. It is important not to lose or obscure the lessons or benefits of the experience. In other words, if a person is going through a challenge and the only goal is to release him or her from the challenge or find a way to make them comfortable, then that person will remain the same throughout the adversity. They are made better off in one situation only to be worse off in those that may follow because nothing about them has fundamentally changed.

Am I saying that I want a person who is in a challenging situation and excruciating emotional pain to continue to feel that pain? No. What I am saying, however, is that in any attempts to help that person, it is imperative that their own growth is not hindered nor their own self-development weakened. The idea is to show them their own inner resources and power. Otherwise, when that person is faced with another challenge, they may not have learned how to access their own strengths, gifts and talents.

In the midst of challenges and adversity we should strive to enable people rather than disable them. It is much like the German playwright, Johann Wolfgang von Goethe, said, "If I accept you as you are, I will make you worse: however, if I treat you as though you are what you are capable of becoming, I help you become that."

In my legal practice, I represented a woman who had just lost her husband. Joanne and Tom had been married over forty years. Tom died from a terminal illness as Joanne approached her sixtieth birthday. He had handled and controlled most of their assets and had done so to their financial detriment. It took well over a year to sort out all of the legal issues and straighten out much of the fiscal damage he had caused to their material worth and her self-worth.

For much of the first six months, I handled all the phone calls, correspondence and court documents necessary to probate Tom's estate. I also took care of many of the personal matters that had come about. Once all the proper documentation was filed with the court, we were able to close the estate and there was little need for further legal representation. However, throughout the course of our professional relationship, Joanne became accustomed to me handling many areas of her personal and business affairs. If I had chosen to continue, I would have temporarily eased her pain and insecurities as I did immediately following the death of her husband. I would have also disabled and disempowered her. My actions would have been a temporary fix that would have positioned her at a disadvantage in the long run. Joanne was now in a place where she could grow from the challenge of losing her husband by accessing and owning her own power. By encouraging her to take control of her life, Joanne developed the confidence in her decisions and abilities to manage her affairs. She then took the next step and re-created her life. Today, Joanne is a very vibrant, independent woman living each day with poise and passion.

I represented another woman whose decisions took her life on a directly opposite path. Bonnie's challenge involved unfair treatment in the workplace. The ordeal resulted in the loss of her job and the loss of her Self. She came to me to sue her employer to recover monetary damages. That was doable. What I could not do, however, was help her recover and reclaim her life.

It took many months for the preliminary investigation into the matter. It took many more years to take the matter to trial. During that time, Bonnie went into a mental and physical downward spiral. She began abusing alcohol and drugs and became involved in highly abusive relationships. She was admitted to several different rehabilitation units. Each time she was discharged, however, Bonnie returned to her previous destructive behaviors.

I received calls from Bonnie at all hours of the day and night asking for help. Although I attempted to guide and direct her, I realized that she was becoming dependent on my presence in her life. I tried to find counseling for her to address the issues that were catapulting her out of control. My attempts were futile. Bonnie made the choice to delve further into her darkness and despair. Being a victim was now her identity.

When we won her case, I had anticipated that there would be emotional recovery and healing taking place on some level. A jury listened, heard and believed her after years of her employer ignoring and denying her claims. However, she was so self-absorbed in her victim mentality that to release it would be to lose her identity and the uniqueness that she had come to believe defined her individuality.

Months after trial and settlement, Bonnie continued to call me crying hysterically. She was in such a critical emotional state that she didn't want guidance or counseling. I attempted to introduce her to professionals that would assist her in regaining her mental health. I also tried to bring in financial advisors to protect her financial health. She refused to follow my counsel in either matter. Bonnie wanted me to somehow, supernaturally, remove her from her self-imposed hell without doing any work herself or taking responsibility for what had become of her life. I was not equipped personally or professionally to do so.

Unlike my other client who used her challenge to grow, this woman allowed her adversity to destroy her life and her whole being. Bonnie wanted the instant gratification of being removed from her situation and someone to do the work for her. Months after winning her lawsuit, she left one abusive relationship only to enter another. She continued to use drugs and got arrested. She lost her house to foreclosure. Due to poor business deals and greedy acquaintances, she spent the rest of the money that we recovered from the lawsuit.

"What does not kill me makes me stronger."
— *Johann Wolfgang von Goethe*

This quote from Goethe could be the marketing slogan and advertising campaign for dealing with adversity. The strength, empowerment and lessons that you gather from each challenge allow you to become more resilient for the next adversity you may encounter.

When you experience the loss of a spouse from death or divorce, the loss of your job or unfair treatment in the workplace, a natural disaster that takes your home or a serious illness that has taken authority over your body, it is difficult to think, 'I will grow and develop from this experience. I will be stronger for having gone through this.' Sometimes you are fortunate enough to be released or removed from the situation and the emotional or physical pain is no longer the constant reminder of the challenge. For the most part, however, you must continue the process of going through the challenge.

The circumstances I have gone through have made me grow and develop spiritually, mentally and emotionally. I have an inner knowing that through my faith and abilities, I can handle anything that this day may bring. I know that I can Shift the Power and access the resources not only to go through but to make it through as well. I know that I will not only survive, but thrive!

In the previous chapter, I briefly described the life altering challenges that were put into motion by Hurricane Charley. These events were just the highlights of what I referred to as my daily crisis of the day.

After living in a motor home for fourteen months, I asked my husband to leave due to his inability to: first, be a husband and, second, be a contractor. The rebuilding process was less than 30% complete when he left and I had no idea how I was going to finish the house. All I knew was that as a contractor my husband wasn't getting the job done and the work wasn't being completed correctly. His inability to handle the challenge made him controlling and emotionally abusive. My marriage affected me and the health and well-being of my parents, who lived on the same property. I could no longer afford the physical and emotional toll. My mother was still recovering from a stroke and my father faced chemotherapy and radiation. Twelve years earlier when Andrew struck, my mother and I had rebuilt. Having overcome that challenge, I knew that it could be done again.

I sat on the bathroom floor with my head in my hands and tears streaming down my face. Looking at the construction debris scattered around the property, the shoddy workmanship that had been performed and the amount of work left to do, I had no idea where I was going to find workmen to complete the job. Although I was at a low point, I remembered how I had dealt with past challenges. I had beat anorexia, recovered from Hurricane Andrew, and been a caretaker of a disabled, brain-damaged parent. I knew the resources that had gotten me through each of the previous challenges and I knew that I could call on them to get me through this.

Most of us do not like change or challenges that impact our lives. We fear it and resist it. The stages of reaction to adversity are much like the stages that you encounter in the grieving process. There is the initial shock that questions the reality of what is happening. This is followed by denial and anger. Oftentimes, anger turns to guilt and we are immobilized by what we should have, could have or would have done. If we sink deeper into feelings of guilt and helplessness, depression can take control of our minds. Once we accept that adversity, transitions and challenges are a part of living, the fear becomes less powerful. Healing and hope can then begin to evolve through the pain.

I got up off the bathroom floor and created a plan by incorporating each of the *PowerShifts* into my daily routine. Each day now began by shifting the power from a spiritual perspective through Prayer and meditation. I did not know how I would find people to work on the house. Being vindictive, my husband was not about to allow anyone of his subcontractors to assist me. I also did not know the outcome of my father's cancer treatments. There was no other option but to give all my worries to God and cast my cares on Him. I was more than willing to do so, knowing from previous experiences that to attempt to take care of all of these things by my own volition would be exhausting and futile.

I took authority over the negative Words and Thoughts that attempted to prevent me from succeeding. Each morning I woke up at 5:00 a.m. For two hours, I read scripture or a positive inspirational book along with my prayer and meditation. During these early morning hours, my mind Focused on scriptures that reinforced a Higher Power that would see me through the adversities. He had never failed me. This morning ritual kept my Words and Thought Focused on things above instead of those below.

I Prayed without ceasing throughout the day. I received a message during one of my Prayer and meditation sessions which told me to wait to dissolve my marriage and file for divorce. My husband and I were separated and rarely spoke to one another. He refused to go to counseling. On one occasion when we spoke, I became so upset with him that I thought to myself that I should just file for divorce so I could start to heal. A voice from within very clearly reprimanded me, saying, 'I told you to wait. You will heal and then you will file.'

I also *Shifted the Power* by surrounding myself with a strong, supportive group of loving and encouraging friends. My Partners allowed me to share my fears and tears without wallowing in self-pity or sinking into the depths of depression. I eliminated toxic people from my life. There were people that enjoyed gossiping and sharing the exploits of my ex-husband. This information was not going to have a positive effect on my life or the task at hand and I didn't need to hear it. I had a job to do and I needed a healthy environment in which to do it. I called on my business coach to assist me in returning to both the business of living and doing business, as well. Her involvement in this process was productive because she prevented me from mentally beating myself up for not accomplishing more of my professional goals during this time. She understood that I was in a state of survival and setting business goals would set me up for failure. She also encouraged me to celebrate my strengths and achievements.

In order to move forward in my personal life, I had to invoke the *PowerShift* of Forgiveness. I needed to release the negative feelings that existed between my husband and me whether or not he chose to do so himself. Also, I had to forgive certain friends and business associates that seemed to want to sabotage my relationship with my husband. I forgave the hurricane. I forgave myself.

Time and energy were premium resources and I became focused. I took care of myself physically through rest, diet and exercise. The previous fourteen months had taken a toll on my immune system. During this period I caught the flu, developed migraine headaches, caught strep throat, and developed an ulcer. My energy was low and I was totally exhausted. I made an effort to get sleep and allow my body to rest and heal. I watched my diet and insured that I received proper nutrition. And, in an effort to reduce stress and increase my energy level, I began working out again by walking, biking and lifting light weights.

Embracing a mood of Gratitude, I felt thankful for my father's recovery, even though he had just begun his treatments. I was grateful for my mother's health as she recovered from her stroke. I was grateful for the people who were guided onto my path to work on the house and I was grateful for the strength and well-being to face each day with renewed determination.

The twelve months that followed were not without obstacles, but I came out on the other side a stronger person and with my self-respect and integrity intact. My mother regained her health. After his treatments, my father had no signs of cancer in his body. The house was 90% complete and I hosted holiday celebrations. I filed for divorce in the spring and, at the time of doing so, had regained my self-esteem and self-empowerment that I had relinquished in my marriage.

In quiet moments of reflection I thought, 'What a difference a year makes.' The previous challenges in my life gave me experience, an adversity resume, so to speak. The *PowerShifts* allowed me to tune out the external noise and chaos and rediscover my inner power and resources. They enabled me to face and overcome adversity to thrive once again.

"There are two ways to live your life. One is as though nothing is a miracle. The other is as though everything is a miracle."

— *Albert Einstein*

At some point in our lives, we are all confronted with challenges that alter our paths. Challenges can change who we are as well. Adversity can be so intense that, at times, we may be overwhelmed and the suffering becomes unbearable. However, it is also a place that is rich with potential for transformation and self-development. We must have the faith and courage to embrace the challenge rather than attempt to resist or run from it. This transformation can present opportunities that were obscured or denied when we were in a comfort or safe zone. It is a place where we go deep within to find our inner resources, call on our faith and use our God-given gifts and talents. In embracing our circumstances, we have the opportunity to embrace our physical life and strengthen our spiritual connection to God.

The chapters that follow will be a journey of discovery. These pages will describe the tools of *The PowerShift Principle* that will assist you through your passage. This is the place where miracles can happen! This is the place where you create a life of purpose, master goals, manifest dreams, accept your significance and realize your greatness. This is the place where the *PowerShifts*!

PowerShift Reflection - Challenges and transitions are inevitable. Release your resistance and give up your need and demand to fully understand their existence. All you need to know is that in the process of this adversity or change, your attitude, your way of being, and your life can transform in ways you never dreamed possible!

CHAPTER
ChREE

POWERSHIFT: PURPOSE, GOALS, AND DREAMS

"For I know the plans I have for you," says the LORD. They are plans for good and not for disaster, to give you a future and a hope."
—*Jeremiah 29:11 (NLT)*

Living your life in Purpose is to live your life with inspiration, creativity, talents and skills. Purpose is discovering the gifts that were specifically designed for you by your Creator to bring forth and share with the physical world. Realizing your Purpose requires you to draw on your spiritual energies and acknowledge your self-empowerment. Challenges and adversity oftentimes serve as catalysts to the realization of your Purpose by requiring you to engage your own power and tap into hidden gifts. Fully embraced, Purpose generates a surge of inner power and energy. This momentum continues to produce even greater inspiration, creativity, talent and skill.

It is easy to distinguish those who are living their life's design in Purpose. They are authentic. They have come to know who they are and do not base their self-worth on the whims of the physical world. Their words and actions emanate from a place of an inner-knowing rather than from the self-importance of the ego. Although their lives are not free of challenges and adversities, their Purpose gives them the resources to overcome the tests and trials. They have no question that their existence has meaning and recognize their significance in the presence of the Creator.

For some, there is a need to make a metaphysical mission out of finding their life's Purpose. They pose it in the form of a cosmic question and believe that there is some definitive answer that must be revealed before they can proceed on their path.

The realization of Purpose is an inner, spiritual journey that inspires a process of growth and discovery through life's experiences. Although we may try to make it more complicated in the physical world, it is a single step onto a path that will guide you thousands of miles on an internal quest.

Living in Purpose and embracing your significance is your birthright. We were made in the image of a perfect Creator and we are more than mere physical beings on a physical planet. The fundamental nature of your Purpose is based on the Dreams in your heart, the visions in your soul and the whisper in your ear. It is what gives life to your spirit. Your Purpose empowers, enlightens and energizes you. It tells you that there is something more, that you are something more. Purpose makes you the participant in your life rather than a bystander. Purpose is a *PowerShift*.

There are three key elements that I believe are imperative to the realization of your Purpose…your Dreams, your Goals and your faith. Each has a unique role. Although they can exist and perform independently, they develop an intimate reliance on one another in the realization of your Purpose. As they work together towards Purpose, they create a sense of harmony which pervades your life.

THREE KEY ELEMENTS TO
REALIZE YOUR PURPOSE

• DREAMS

• GOALS

• FAITH

*"I dream my painting and
then I paint my dream."*
—*Vincent Van Gogh*

Dreams

Dreams represent the vision of the life that you want to lead. They exist in your mind's eye as an expression of who you truly are and how you want to create your life. They are the reach for the stars type desires and imagery that you see and experience in those moments when you shut out the physical world. We daydream as children and those daydreams transform into games of make-believe on the playground. In those innocent periods of play and pretend, we are rock stars and rodeo riders, astronauts and explorers. We are discovering the great unknown and, without knowing it, we are discovering ourselves.

DREAMS ARE THE COMPASS FOR YOUR SOUL

How can you live your life in Purpose? Return to your Dreams. Dreams are the compass for your soul. As adults, the gravity of our responsibilities and the importance of the self that we portray in order to accomplish and become successful takes our Dreams and tucks them deep within our minds. We do this in part to keep from failing, to keep from getting hurt and to fit into a mold that has been dictated either by our family or society. We manipulate our external personality for our family, clients and friends, minimizing the desire to Dream and losing the desire to play. Disregarding our Dreams, we may allow others to impose their desires on us and dictate what we should be. Often, we allow the circumstances surrounding challenges and adversity to negatively drive the direction of our lives. And yet, there is that voice or vision awaiting acknowledgement to be set free. Once you liberate your Dreams, they will ignite the life in your spirit and the spirit in your life.

Goals

The second element of realizing your Purpose is Goals. Goals have the ability to direct your Dreams and make them the star of a life-enhancing, passion-infused production. Dreams are the conception. Goals are the birthing process. Dreams unleash the creative life force within. Goals are the fuel behind that vital force. Dreams give your Goals the wings needed to fly. Goals give your Dreams the landing gear to bring them into reality. Dreams and Goals have the energy to keep you pressing forward despite your situation or the obstacles that you face and shift you in the direction of your Purpose.

*"So I run straight to the goal
with purpose in every step."*
— *1 Corinthians 9:26*

Goals play a vital part in the realization of your Purpose. They are also the most misunderstood element. Goal is definitely a four letter word because it can strike fear in your heart and self-loathing in your soul. The sound of the word "goal" itself can, at times, create anxiety and apprehension. Anxiety and apprehension sometimes block the flow of positive energy needed to reach for your Dreams. You may be reminded of past failures, disappointments and letdowns and, in turn, your reaction produces a fear of future failures, disappointment and letdowns. This negative invasive force can quickly extinguish the passion of your Dreams' performance.

How can you overcome this negative force? Goals are not the end of your journey! They are the road map. Along the way, there may be detours that take you down a different road and give you a greater perspective of where you are traveling. You may encounter a super highway where things pick up speed, or you may run into a bumpy dirt road to slow you down. There are rest stops to refuel and recharge. You might even find some great tourist attractions where you can learn and play. The trip is yours to take.

To get started, let's review the basics to setting your Goals:

First: Your Goals must include short-term Goals and long-term Goals.

Second: You must be specific.

Third: You must write them down.

Fourth: You must state them in the positive and affirm them both mentally and verbally.

Fifth: You must define a time-line for their achievement.

All these actions support your physical being in attaining your Goals. They also serve to focus your mental energies on your desires. These are excellent time-tested techniques which have allowed many people to succeed in their endeavors. Unfortunately, they have also caused many to give up on their Dreams and to give up on themselves. They can manifest feelings of failure instead of success and thoughts of disappointment instead of accomplishment. These tools are lacking in an important component. They fail to fully emphasize and embrace the assistance and support of the spiritual being.

Faith

"Now faith is the substance of things hoped for, the evidence of things not seen."
— Hebrews 11:1(NKJV)

If your Dreams are the star of your life's production and your Goals are the director, then Faith is the producer. Faith gives you the determination and the resilience to continue to pursue the production of your Dreams and Goals even if the audience isn't buying the tickets and the critics are panning the show. It is an unshakable belief in God, and a conviction within, that generates the power and the energy to follow your heart and soul despite the reviews.

"Don't copy the behavior and customs of this world, but let God transform you into a new person by changing the way you think. Then you will learn to know God's will for you, which is good and pleasing and perfect."

— *Romans 12:2 (NLT)*

Your Purpose is God's will for you. Your Dreams and Goals are the tools which He uses to develop your wisdom and gain the experience necessary to step fully into your Purpose. The process requires the constant reinforcement of your spiritual and mental being. In order to provide the support to realize and embrace your Purpose, master your Goals and manifest your Dreams, remember that your Purpose is MADE in HEAVEN.

Meditate	**Heed**
Affirm	**Enjoy**
Detach	**Activate**
Empower	**Visualize**
	Entrust
	Neutralize

Meditation

"Whatever things are true, whatever things are noble, whatever things are just, whatever things are pure, whatever things are lovely, whatever things are of good report, if there is any virtue and if there is anything praiseworthy—meditate on these things."
— *Philippians 4:8 (NKJV)*

The first step in Goal-mastering is Meditation. Meditation is a practice of quieting the mind, relaxing the body and entering into a realm of spiritual awareness. The physical and mental body rests while your soul aligns with your sense of Purpose. It is a time to tune out all the noise of the day, the noise in your mind and reconnect with God. If prayer is our chance to talk to God, then meditation is God's opportunity to speak with us.

One reason why people don't meditate is because they are afraid of the silence and afraid of what God may have to say to them. Or, they think that it is too difficult. We live in a world that now requires multi-tasking. Our minds are inundated with images and sounds from cell phones, televisions, computers, radio, media and other means of stimulus. We are conditioned to live on sensory overload.

One day I was walking on the treadmill in the gym when I realized that I was watching three different televisions on closed caption, listening to the music playing throughout the facility and catching up on my reading by thumbing through a magazine. And the idea of exercising is to maintain health and reduce stress! People have difficulty quieting their minds because of the constant barrage of junk and outside noise that we receive in the form of other people's thoughts and ideas. Meditation reduces the influence of the physical world and returns the control over your thoughts to you.

Many believe that the practice of meditation takes hours each day and years to get it right. They just can't squeeze it into their daily schedule. They imagine a guru spending hours on a mountainside in a trance oblivious to the world about them. Others have tried to sit still and be quiet only to consistently battle the thoughts that pop into their heads. They become more irritated instead of relaxed. There are many different methods to meditate and there is no right or wrong way to enter into this state. You may begin by setting aside ten minutes each day to close your eyes and allow your mind and body to benefit from the stillness. Breathe in slowly and say to yourself, "I breathe in peace now." As you slowly exhale, say to yourself, "I release all stress now." Release all expectations as to what you will experience. When the day's thoughts enter your mind, acknowledge them and allow them to gently leave your being.

"Be still and know that I am God."
— *Psalm 46:10(NLT)*

PowerShift Reflection - As the brain-babble relinquishes its hold over the mental state, the mind can surrender to your higher self. This is where you reconnect with the Divine and recharge your inner resources and power. You receive answers and guidance. In the stillness, your life's design can be tweaked or the plan revealed on a grander scale. Dreams become real and Goals are mastered before they manifest in the physical world.

Affirmations

"O Lord, what great works you do!
And how deep are your thoughts."
— *Psalm 92:5 (NLT)*

Control your thoughts and you control your Power. By managing your mind, you can direct the situations surrounding challenges and transitions rather than reacting to them. Affirmations are a way to reclaim your thoughts and gain authority over your mind. They are positive, constructive statements that have the ability to reprogram your subconscious as you consciously change your way of thinking.

The key to effective affirmations is to use statements that resonate with your mind, body and soul. If a phrase causes any conflict or intense doubts as you speak it, you may not fully receive the intended results or benefits. You may need to take the affirmation process in steps, beginning with basic phrases. Then develop and advance your affirmations as you cultivate greater confidence in your abilities to achieve and succeed. Choose words and statements that will reinforce your Goals and Dreams.

I have created affirmative statements which are personal to me and have also used scriptures that support my Dreams and Goals. At times, I have merged the two. I will share with you one of my favorite affirmations that I speak daily. The words are borrowed from the 23rd Psalm. If these words hold positive meaning for you, you may use them as well.

The Lord is my shepherd, my guardian, my guide.
All of my needs, wants, desires, goals and prayers manifest in Divine order.
He restores my soul and renews my spirit.
He leads me on my path and purpose to greatness in His glorious name.
And though I may face challenges along the way,
I meet them with success and confidence.
For I know that he is with me.
His loving hand strengthens and supports me in the Love and the Light.
He fills my life with an abundance of peace, love, joy, laughter,
Success, happiness, and prosperity,
He aligns me in the Divine Spirit of the Christ Consciousness,
My blessings continue to multiply.
Surely greatness shall surround me all the days of my life,
And I shall walk hand in hand with the Lord, my God, forever.

Affirmations must be personal to you and they must be in alignment with where you are physically, mentally and spiritually. You must create them for yourself and use them. Write them on sticky notes and place them around your house. Post them in your car. Write them on index cards and review them every time you have a few moments. Record your affirmations and listen to them during your meditation. Allow them to touch and penetrate all of your physical, mental and spiritual senses.

PowerShift Reflection - Affirmations bring the spiritual into the physical. Affirmative physical statements enhance your intuitive experience and transfer your Purpose from the subconscious to the conscious state. The inner knowing of who you are is made manifest by speaking these positive thoughts. They assist in the creation of the PowerShift and clear the mind to allow you to master your Goals, manifest your Dreams and live in Purpose.

Detachment

"But let patience have its perfect work, that you may be perfect and complete, lacking nothing."
— James 1:4 (NKVJ)

The greatest gift of your Goals and Dreams is who you become in the process of achieving them. God is much more interested in the person we become, rather than how fast we get there and how much stuff we have accumulated in the process. To that end, you must detach yourself from the outcome. This may sound like a paradox, but Goals and Dreams are dynamic. As they cause you to grow and mature, they also grow and mature. It is a cyclical effect. During the process of achievement, you may no longer be the same person that wanted to accomplish a specific Goal and that Goal may no longer hold significance for you. That change, in and of itself, may have been the reason for the Goal in the first place, to stimulate a transformation in you.

One of the early Goal-setting techniques requires that you set a definite time for its accomplishment. I agree that the physical mind needs boundaries so that it doesn't wander without direction. However, if you fail to meet that deadline, you may feel like you have failed or missed the mark. A moment in physical time which you have set for yourself may not be the one set for you by God.

How do you know when to go after your Dreams? The answer is within you. That perfect timing is between you and God. There may be a period where there is a learning curve and you need to become something more from a spiritual or physical basis in order to be prepared for all that God has set out before you. That moment is also between you and God.

For example, I knew that I had books to write. I knew that I was being called by God to transform people's lives. I saw the vision in my mind's eye and felt it throughout my being. When I began to write, I was interrupted. It wasn't a phone call or a knock at the door. These were life interruptions, like a major family illness or a catastrophic hurricane. These disruptions took my life off track. My Dreams and life vision were placed on hold, time and again. I became frustrated and tired. At one point, I wondered if God was trying to tell me something. I questioned whether I had misunderstood or, worse yet, if I had missed my opportunity.

God pointed out to me that I was changing and working in people's lives in my law practice, one client at a time. It wasn't the original vision that I had, but I was living my life in Purpose. I was growing and transforming by the research that I continued to do, my professional work, the personal study and the daily experiences in my life.

The opportunity to teach and write presented itself once more. I reviewed what I wrote prior to the challenges that had invaded my life. Since then, I had been presented with the opportunity for more growth, knowledge and empathy. I had experienced so many more things since I had first started to write and teach. There was nothing wrong with what I had written, but it wasn't my Purpose. God had taken the time to ensure that I was the person He wanted me to be prior to stepping further into my Goals and Dreams, and further onto my path of Purpose.

PowerShift Reflection - Dreams and Goals may appear in your mind's eye and you may feel them in your heart and soul. However, you may not possess the physical or mental maturity or sufficient spiritual awareness to support their birth into the physical realm. You must first grow into the person who can sustain these Dreams. You must honor the process and detach from the outcome. In doing so, you grow into your Purpose.

Empowerment

"Stand firm in the faith. Be courageous. Be strong."
— 1 Corinthians 16:13(NLT)

Empowerment is a necessary energy to the attainment of your Goals. You must maintain a genuine belief in yourself and a steadfast belief in your Dreams. Mastering your Goals and stepping into your Purpose requires that you explore unknown and unfamiliar territory. Navigating new terrain demands that you refine familiar skills and develop new and additional resources. Calling on untried skills can create anxiety and fear. Left unattended, these negative emotions can paralyze you and block your abilities to bring your Goals and Dreams into reality.

Fear has been called false evidence appearing real. In order to enter evidence at trial you must establish its authenticity. A set of questions must be asked and answered appropriately as proof of the legitimacy of the evidence. Most of the time, that which you fear is not authentic and could not pass such a test. There is no basis in reality for its existence. In order to conquer your fears you must be secure with your inner power. Say "I can and I will do this!"

The very essence of your soul is greatness. You were created in the image of a perfect Creator. You have a destiny to manifest. Therefore, why should you ever doubt your abilities and your aptitudes to achieve your Dreams and Goals? Does your ego fill your mind with mistrust and uncertainty? Do skepticism and self-criticism erode your self-confidence and downplay your Dreams? Do you point out your own shortfalls and allow your innate greatness to become obscured in thoughts of fear? If you have answered "yes" to any of these questions, the true nature of your soul has risked the possibility of being rejected.

I have encountered several occasions in my life when I relinquished my power and was so overwhelmed by fear that it threatened my Goals and Dreams. During my first year of law school, I was afflicted with what I call the *imposter syndrome*. This syndrome is not a physically life-threatening disorder. However, it can mentally cripple and destroy Dreams. I walked around campus thinking that I didn't belong and wasn't good enough to become an attorney. I felt like I didn't fit in, yet I put on a happy face and worried that I would be discovered as a fraud.

There was no basis for my thought process. I had graduated from college with honors and had a great deal of life experience before attending law school. Inner logic argued that I passed the entrance exams and had been accepted at the university on my own merits. However, an unrelenting voice in my head told me that I wasn't enough. The voice became so loud that occasionally I became physically ill before my class during my first year.

I was in new territory. Law school is not only about knowledge but it also retrains your thought process to develop analytical skills. As an undergrad, learning came easy and I expected to be able to maintain the same level of comprehension. I spent so much additional time studying that I thought I wasn't smart enough. Finally, someone put it into perspective for me. They said that law school was like a bad cold. I would feel miserable for the duration but I would live through it. They also said that, for the most part, the law wasn't that complicated because most attorneys aren't geniuses. My perception shifted and there was less anxiety in my second year. I graduated, passed my state bar and became a practicing attorney. In retrospect, I wasted much energy. This thinking stole my joy, peace and power.

PowerShift Reflection - Hindsight is always a better judge of the situation. When you deal with fear in the present, call an immediate stop to all of your negative images. Shift your perception to the positive. Empower yourself through your relationship with God, knowing that your Dreams and Goals are gifts from your Creator. You have all that you need and lack nothing.

Heed

> *"Seek the Kingdom of God above all else, and live*
> *righteously, and He will give you everything you need."*
> — *Matthew 6:33(NLT)*

While mastering your Goals and manifesting your Dreams, you may need to redirect and refocus. There may come a time in the midst of challenges that you must shift direction and concentrate your energies in another area. Heed that inner voice or that gnawing sensation in your gut saying that a change is in order. This is part of the growing process into Purpose. Be willing to listen to your Higher Power. Make the necessary course corrections even if you think that you are still headed in the right direction.

Above all, your Goals and Dreams must remain congruent with your Purpose. Detours off the projected path may actually serve your Purpose. However, you must use your Divine Guidance system to monitor your progress and warn you if the deviations are not in alignment with your life's design. If you do things for the wrong reasons, you may still accomplish Goals, but they will not allow you to experience the significance you seek or to step fully into your Purpose.

I had a friend with a phenomenal gift for achieving all that he set out to accomplish. Richard saw it in his mind and his Focus became a beacon attracting everything and everybody he needed into his life to attain his Goals. He was the textbook example for the law of attraction. Richard achieved all of his material Goals: the bank account, the retirement account, a Porsche in the garage, and a four bedroom house in an upscale gated community. He got all of the toys and traveled and dined at the places to be seen. However, for all of his material wealth and possessions, his life remained empty. There was a void. All of the things that he thought would create happiness only left him in search for something more to fill the barren place in his soul.

Richard's Goals had no spiritual basis or higher Purpose. There had been a point in his life when he could have achieved his Goals and maintained his spiritual integrity. He could have lived his life fully in Purpose and achieved the significance that would have satisfied his soul. However, he failed to heed that inner-voice and listen to its wisdom. Material success was at hand and he wasn't willing to modify his course. Consequently, Richard achieved only to satisfy his ego and without concern for others he might affect in the process.

Self-gratification, based solely on ego-gratification, leads to an absence of joy and satisfaction. He hurt people who cared for him and attracted the companionship of false friends. His empty achievements and deflated Dreams led him to an addiction to drugs and alcohol in an effort to numb the pain. His health and his reputation were irreparably damaged.

PowerShift Reflection - As you master your Goals, always ask for guidance from God and acknowledge that you will receive the His support. Respect your intuition. Listen to that still, small voice in your ear. Trust that feeling in your gut.

Enjoy

"...for the joy of the Lord is your strength."
— *Nehemiah 8:10 (NLT)*

It is our birthright to experience joy and peace. Our Goals, Dreams and life's Purpose are intended to create joy and make our existence in the physical realm richer and more satisfying. Christ said that He came so that we may have and enjoy life and have it to the full. (John 10:10 NIV) It is not our fate to trudge through each day disgruntled, disappointed and anxious.

When you enjoy the process of mastering your Goals, it impresses upon your subconscious mind that your Goals and Dreams are definite and worthwhile things. When joy fills your unconscious mind, there is energy released throughout your being. This spiritually magnetic power draws to you that which you need to bring your Dreams into fruition.

There are several points to keep in mind when joy seems to be absent from the Goal-mastering process. First, reevaluate what you want to accomplish to make sure that the Goals and Dreams are yours. You cannot live someone else's life, nor can you accomplish their Dreams. Sometimes we think that allowing another to live vicariously through our achievements is honorable. It actually dishonors both yours and the other person's Dreams as well. Their Dreams and Goals are for them to achieve.

There are other times when we have not yet formed the specifics of our Goals and Dreams. We become open and susceptible to the suggestions that others may have for us. My undergraduate experience in college is a case-in-point. I jokingly refer to my curriculum as the eight-year-eight college plan. In high school, I entertained thoughts of becoming a veterinarian. As is the case with most high school students, circumstances occurred to change my mind and I went in search of a different major and career path. As I have said earlier, guidance counselors encouraged me to apply to a number of colleges and universities. I wanted to attend a community college for a few semesters and remain close to my family and horses. Knowing that I wanted to complete a college degree but having no definitive idea of what I wanted to do left me open to everyone's opinions. The results were eight years, eight colleges, and five majors. I finally graduated from the University of Miami, eight years after my graduation from high school. In my defense, I was forced to withdraw for three years as a result of my father's illness.

It was during that time, however, that I was able to step back and decide what it was that I wanted for me. I had not enjoyed my college experience. I did not enjoy my majors. My lack of direction for my life took me on a detour where I attempted to fit into some preconceived notion of what other people thought that I should become or do with my life. Their thoughts were not my Goals and Dreams. At point in my life, I was both too intimidated by my own Dreams and too afraid of letting other people down. The absence of joy should have been an indication that I was not in my own Goal-mastering or Dream-manifesting process.

Joy is also absent when people become discouraged because they are not where they want or think they should be at any given moment in their lives. Joy motivates us. We are the Dream masters and we thrive in the enjoyment of the passion to accomplish our Dreams. Challenges, adversity, interruptions, other people, time and our own thoughts can all devalue our Dreams and deceive us into thinking that we will never accomplish our Goals. If you find yourself at this place, take the time to reevaluate where you are as opposed to where you think you should be and why you think you should be there. Once you do, you may be closer to achieving your Dreams and realizing your Purpose than you think.

During a conversation on career opportunities, a friend shared with me that if he had the opportunity to start over again he would become a doctor. He wanted to make a difference and save peoples' lives. Frank retired after serving 25 years with the New York Police Department. As our discussion continued, he recounted stories of some of the people he had helped during his tenure of service: the child he held waiting for paramedics when her arm had been severed, the woman he rescued from a hostage situation and the kid on the streets who just needed someone to listen to him. Many times, he had placed his own life on the line to save people in life-threatening situations. By the time he finished telling his stories, he realized that he had actually achieved his Dreams by influencing and saving lives.

PowerShift Reflection - Are you, at this moment, actually serving your Purpose and realizing your Dreams? Take a moment to see and enjoy the process.

Activate

"*Therefore, prepare your minds for action.*"
— *1 Peter 1:13 (NIV)*

All the planning, strategies, talent and skills will lead you nowhere unless you activate and implement them. Taking action claims your authority over your Goals and Dreams. It transforms your Dreams from their state of being within your heart and mind's eye into reality. Taking action transforms your Goals from intangible desires to tangible results.

As simple as this may sound, this is the stage at which many get stuck in the manifestation process. Some are great visionaries, but lack the inner means and motivation to act upon their visions. Some are so overwhelmed by the magnitude of their Goals and Dreams that they paralyze their energies. Some people feel that they must know everything about a particular subject in order to proceed. They become stuck in a quest for further knowledge that can cause their Goals and Dreams to stagnate. Then there are those who simply do not know where to start.

Indecisiveness and inaction drain energy and allow people to succumb to mediocrity. You must remember that God does not place a Dream in your heart without giving you the substance to fulfill it. You are His creation and His child. He will meet you at your level of action. Yes, there are unanswered Dreams. And, there are many people who fail to take that necessary first step to draw the energy into their presence to sustain their Dreams and Goals.

Not all actions are going to produce great results. Twenty-percent of your actions will produce eighty-percent of your results. Undoubtedly, you will screw up, mess up and get it wrong. Remember, in God's plan there are no design flaws. Redirect, refocus and reenergize, but continue to take action.

"Whatever you do or dream you can do – begin it.
Boldness has genius and power and magic in it."
— *Johann Wolfgang von Goethe*

Where do you start the activation process? I like the words of Lewis Carroll in the childhood classic *Adventures of Alice in Wonderland*. "Begin at the beginning," the King said, very gravely, "and go on till you come to the end; then stop."

> *PowerShift Reflection - Break down your Goals and Dreams into their individual and separate processes. Outline the actions necessary to complete each stage. Then take one step at a time. You will be amazed at the large strides you will make in achieving your Dreams when you start with one small step.*

Visualization

"Where there is no vision, the people perish."
— *Proverbs 29:18 (KJV)*

You must first visualize your Dreams and Goals in your mind's eye before they manifest in the physical world. Through visualization, you will bring your Goals and Dreams to life. Visualization stimulates the energy to attract to you that which you imagine. Envisioning your Goals and Dreams as already achieved creates a force and power that will usher them into existence.

Visualization works because your mind does not know the difference between reality and perception. Performance coaches know the value of making their students practice through visualization. It is the only playing field where you can practice perfectly, over and over again.

I used this technique with my students when I taught horseback riding. In dressage, the horse and rider must perform a test in a ring by themselves. They are scored by the judge for each movement. Many of my students had limited time to ride because of school and work. I had them ride the test in their minds each night before they went to sleep. This became the show ring where their ride and riding skills were flawless. Visualizing a perfect performance allowed their abilities, confidence and scores to improve with each competition.

> *PowerShift Reflection – Visualize your Goals and Dreams as accomplished. Be specific as to each detail, no matter how small or seemingly unimportant. Allow the pictures in your mind's eye to generate the energy to manifest your Goals and Dreams in the physical world.*

Entrust

"Commit everything you do to the Lord. Trust him, and He will help you."
—*Psalm 37:5(NLT)*

Dreams, Goals and Purpose are God's gift to you. It has been said that what you do with them are your gift back to God. Your Creator believes in you so much as to give to you the responsibility of your Dreams and Goals. You must, therefore, entrust him with their attainment. Achieving your Dreams and Goals, and realizing your Purpose honors God. Of course He will support you in your endeavors.

"Commit your actions to the Lord,
and your plans will succeed."
— Proverbs 16:3 (NLT)

Entrusting your Dreams to God allows you to find peace and to rest. You do what you can do and allow God to be God. Many times, we pray about our Goals and turn our Dreams over to Him. Then, fifteen minutes later we take them back to become involved in chaotic activity that is totally unproductive. How many times have you had unexpected phone calls, fortuitous meetings or become involved in unforeseen events that in some way led you closer to your Goal? That is how God works, when we allow Him to do so.

A friend of mine had an idea and vision for a business opportunity but he needed to represent the right company in order to implement it. One day as he returned from vacation, he was bumped into first class on his return flight. He overheard the conversation of the man seated in front of him who happened to be the CEO of a company that would benefit from his idea. The introduction and the initial presentation were made between take-off and landing. Shortly thereafter, the idea became reality. Both men benefited greatly from a fortuitous change in seating arrangements.

"The moment one definitely commits oneself, then Providence moves too. All sorts of things occur to help one that would have never otherwise have occurred…unforeseen incidents, meetings and material assistance, which no man could have dreamed would have come his way."
— Johann Wolfgang von Goethe

PowerShift Reflection - Commit your Dreams, Goals and Purpose to God as He has committed them to you. Trust that the right thing will happen at the right time. Know that when a door is closed, a window will open. Don't stand there shaking the locked knob of a door to which you are no longer being granted access. Take the window, or take the stairs, knowing that if God has trusted you with such beautiful Dreams, you can commit your Goals and trust Him to deliver you to the right place at the right time to the right people. Remember…Let God be God.

Neutralize

"Guard your heart above all else, for it determines the course of your life. Avoid all perverse talk; stay away from corrupt speech."
— Proverbs 4:23-24(NLT)

You must protect your Dreams and Goals from the negative energy that exists in the physical world. This destructive energy can come from family, friends, clients, professional associates, media resources and even from you. Neutralizing the negativity is crucial to mastering your Goals, manifesting your Dreams and living in Purpose.

*"I will not let anyone walk through my
mind with dirty feet."*
— *Mahatma Gandhi*

Some people may feel threatened by your Goals and Dreams. They think that if you succeed, it will diminish them. They may send negative thoughts and energy in your direction, saying things to plant seeds of doubt and uncertainty in your mind. They may act deliberately and attempt to sabotage you. Or, they may be totally unaware of their influence or imagine that they are well-meaning. Whether it is intentional or unintentional, the results are the same. Choose carefully those with whom you share your Dreams and Goals, especially in the fragile moments of their inception. Know your inner-circle and those whom you can trust with your life because your Dreams, Goals and Purpose are your life.

You must also neutralize yourself. Moments of discouragement and doubt are common. Sometimes we just want to feel bad, to feel as though we will never accomplish our Goals. We are like a tired child throwing a temper tantrum. We want it all, NOW. However, when we think and speak against our Goals and Dreams we begin to contradict all of our positive work. Much like you would do with a child, give yourself a time-out. Do something to immediately shift your energy into a positive posture.

*PowerShift Reflection - Meditate, pray, say affirmations or go for
a walk to neutralize the negativity that may flood your mind and
flow from your mouth.*

"I am here for a purpose and that purpose is to grow into a mountain, not to shrink to a grain of sand. Henceforth will I apply ALL my efforts to become the highest mountain of all and I will strain my potential until it cries for mercy."
— Og Mandino

Your Purpose is Made in Heaven to manifest on earth through your Goals and Dreams. When you choose to live in Purpose, master your Goals and manifest your Dreams, you choose to create a *PowerShift*!

PowerShift Reflection - The closer that you draw to your Goals and Dreams, the closer you draw to God. The closer you draw to God, the closer you draw to your Purpose. Your Purpose is truly not a metaphysical mission. Nor is it a cosmic question. Your Purpose is the essence of your greatness. It is the gift from your Creator and is supported by your Creator. Your Goals and Dreams are the significance that your spiritual being has chosen to express in the physical world.

CHAPTER
FOUR

POWERSHIFT: PRAYER

"The earnest prayer of a righteous person has great power and produces wonderful results."
— *James 5:16 (NLT)*

The *PowerShift* of Prayer creates a dynamic energy. A consistent practice of Prayer has the ability to create, stimulate and give full force and effect to all the other *PowerShifts*. When you posture yourself in a state of Prayer, you are one with your Creator. You raise your consciousness, enlarge your vision and live in the present moment with your heart open towards God. The draining forces of the physical world are closed out. When your mental, physical and spiritual energies are revitalized and rejuvenated through Prayer, there is a *PowerShift*!

An established Prayer practice is especially important when confronted with life's challenges, transitions and adversities. Prayer allows you to draw on resources greater than your own. Life is full of suddenlys. Suddenly your life changes in an instant. You may be faced with a challenge and overwhelmed with no way to resolve the situation. Although adversity may represent a negative suddenly, Prayer can summon a positive suddenly. Suddenly a person you need is directed into your path. Suddenly an adversarial circumstance turns in your favor. Suddenly, and maybe subtly, your life changes again in an instant.

Prayer, defined simply, is the heart and mind coming together in agreement to connect with God. This union connects to a conscious communication with Him. Prayer, however, is more than just words. Practiced with sincerity, it embraces your heart, motivates your mind, inspires your spirit and empowers your soul. Prayer activates your relationship with God and makes it personal. The more you continue to engage the Divine in Prayer, the more intimate and mature the relationship will become. Your Creator is already well acquainted with you, Prayer allows you to become acquainted with Him. In your Prayer practice, you come to know with absolute certainty that your life is significant because you come to know the One that gave life to your soul.

Prayer generates the inner confidence and conviction to live a high-performance life. Prayer also produces the supernatural resources to see you through any of life's challenges. Through your practice, you can conquer your fears, overcome apathy, and create the enthusiasm to step into the life you have envisioned in your mind's eye. The power of Prayer produces a force which allows you to reclaim your authority over your body, mind and soul. You, essentially, take back the power you gave away to circumstances, challenges or other people in the physical world. Prayer sets the course for doing the right thing, at the right time, for the right reasons. This *Power-Shift* gives you the ability to become a co-creator of your own life with the Creator.

You also begin to recognize the influence of the Divine in your daily life and know that God's hand is in the smallest details to deliver your blessings. You learn that there is no scale on which to judge miracles, blessings and the favor of God. There is not one Divine gift that is any greater than another. You can be witness to a loved one recovering from a serious illness or be grateful for a new job offer. You can appreciate the beauty of a sunflower opening to face the warmth and the light of the sun or stand in awe as you watch a shooting star burning through the heavens. You know that if there is a Higher Power dictating the order of this complex universe, He can certainly manage the affairs of your life.

Despite its benefits, people fail to incorporate this *PowerShift* into their lives. Some hold the belief that they are their own Higher Power and they are fully in charge of their destiny without any outside assistance from another entity. Others believe that Prayer must be formal and doubt that their words or thoughts will be heard by God. They are under the perception that they must pray the right way and in proper format. It becomes too challenging to formulate an eloquent sentence that is worthy of the Creator. Others think that the things for which they pray are not acceptable to God unless they are spiritual. And then there are those people who require instant gratification as proof that Prayer is effective in their lives. If it doesn't happen within their time frame, which is usually immediately or shortly thereafter, then Prayer doesn't work. Other people turn to Prayer only as a last resort when they are in the midst of challenge and adversity.

"I have held many things in my hands, and I have lost them all; but whatever I placed in God's hands, that I still possess."
— *Martin Luther*

There have been many blessings and miracles in my life that can be attributed to the *PowerShift* of Prayer. I have experienced both simple moments of peace and joy, and life-changing events. I have also experienced and witnessed healings. My relationship with God has become stronger and my Prayer practice has deepened as I have grown spiritually. Perhaps I should say that I have grown spiritually because my relationship with God has become stronger and my Prayer practice has deepened.

My Prayer practice has matured and developed through the experiences of my life. However, I have not always felt closeness to my Creator. As a child, the church I attended placed images in my head of a God of wrath, wielding a mighty sword that was ready to strike me down at the first sign of sin. Prayers and creeds were repeated in cadence, fully lacking in enthusiasm or emotion. The words felt empty and meaningless. Hymns were sung in a monotone melody and sounded more like a dirge rather than a joyful noise. It was all about what color candle to light, which color robe to wear and which cross to adorn for the season. As a young adult, it was not appealing to me to have a close relationship with a God who appeared to be superficial and vengeful.

My enlightenment occurred when God intervened and saved me from destroying myself through anorexia. The darkest days of my life allowed the light to come in. The representation of a wrathful God that had invoked fear became the image of a loving God. Once I came to know this presence, nothing could ever separate me from His love. I would never again allow a person or an organization to define my relationship with Him or dictate the manner in which to communicate with Him. The barriers that prevented any spiritual intimacy were removed and a relationship with a Loving Father evolved.

My intention is not to teach you how to pray or to advocate the tenets of a particular religion, but to share the benefit of Prayer experiences that played an integral part in my *PowerShift* during the challenges and adversities that shaped my life. I want to impart what I have learned about Prayer through my relationship to God without disrespecting or alienating any particular religious or spiritual beliefs. Your Prayer practice, as is your relationship with God, is yours to build upon and develop.

"Love to pray. Feel often during the day the need for prayer, and take trouble to pray. Prayer enlarges the heart until it is capable of containing God's gift of Himself. Ask and seek and your heart will grow big enough to receive Him."
— *Mother Teresa*

Prayer is a tool that I use to cultivate the awareness of God in my life. I spend quiet time in Prayer in the mornings. However, I talk to God all through the day. I have come to depend on the scripture in 1 Thessalonians 5:17 (NIV) "pray continually." I pray when a negative thought comes into my mind, prior to meeting with clients, and I pray for others. I also pray when there is something on my mind and it creates havoc with my day. I pray when I am riding, driving and exercising. I stay in a constant state of communication with God. I have found in doing so, He remains in a constant state of communication with me.

I have learned that Prayer does not have to be formal to be effective. The language does not have to be ornate, nor does it need to be translated into the verbiage of the Old English. The setting does not need to be elaborate or in a particular location. Prayer does not have to be in any specific form or for any certain length of time. The manner in which you pray may change over the course of time. Prayer serves you. Your relationship with God alone will determine the parameters of your Prayer practice.

There are two energies that allow Prayer to create a *PowerShift* in your life. First, your Prayer must be from the heart. The words must be sincere and have a purpose. You cannot utter words in the absence of feeling and emotion and expect to get a passionate, supernatural response. The words may be those of thanksgiving or a Prayer of petition. They may be for you or they may be for another. Your Prayer may ask for forgiveness, as well as a healing. It may ask for assistance with a perceived need. The language can be simple and unpretentious. *Forgive me. Heal me. I need. Thank you.* The words, however, must be accompanied by a strong, deep conviction that is found within. Delivered with the authenticity of your spirit, they flow through your lips or mind and create an intention to call upon God and appeal to His awareness.

"Have faith in God. I tell you the truth, you can say to this mountain, 'May you be lifted up and thrown into the sea,' and it will happen. But you must really believe it will happen and have no doubt in your heart. I tell you, you can pray for anything, and if you believe that you've received it, it will be yours."

— *Mark 11: 22 - 24 (NLT)*

The second energy that allows Prayer to create a *PowerShift* in your life is faith. If you want God to do great things in your life, then call on Him in faith. Faith is trust in God. It is a knowing that suspends all doubt that your Prayer has been heard and will be answered. Faith is the confidence in yourself acknowledging that what you have asked is in agreement with the highest and best good of all involved.

During life's challenges, it may be difficult to generate faith. I know that there have been desperate moments when my faith has been less about belief and more about pleading and begging. Fear has become the prevailing energy. Allowed to wander in the mind unrestrained, anxiety and fear suppress faith. When you experience those moments, find ways to overcome the doubts and uncertainties that invade and pollute your mind. Faith is the more powerful of the two energies. Faith has the ability to prevail over fear if you give it the sustenance that it needs to do so.

There are several tools that can fortify faith and alleviate fear. Quoting scripture calls upon God's words and promises and reinforces your faith. When pleading a case before a judge, an attorney supports his premise by presenting corresponding case law and statutes. Statutes are rules and regulations. Case law represents decisions which have been previously handed down. Scripture can be used in the same manner. It contains the laws, agreements and previous decision handed down from God. Citing appropriate scripture presents your case before the ultimate judge using His rules and resolutions. The spiritual force contained in these words intensifies your faith as they become imprinted in your mind.

"And it is impossible to please God without faith. Anyone who wants to come to him must believe that God exists and that he rewards those who sincerely seek him."
— *Hebrews 11:6 (NLT)*

Another technique to develop or strengthen your faith is to make a list of all previously answered Prayers. This inventory catalogs both minor requests and major events that have been changed by the influence of Prayer. Reviewing this list will remind you that you do have clout with the Creator.

He does listen and respond. Your soul will fill with the acknowledgment and joy of the blessings that you previously received. Armed with the knowledge that your Prayers have been answered before, you have the ability to confirm and acknowledge that they will be answered again.

You can also increase your faith by looking at what God has accomplished in the lives of others. This is not done to create envy or inferiority. Reflect on how He has worked in the situation or circumstance of another person. Open your mind's eye and heart and acknowledge that if God has allowed another to realize the answer to their Prayers and petitions, He will do the same for you.

"Devote yourselves to prayer with an alert mind and a thankful heart."
— *Colossians 4:2 (NLT)*

Immediate gratitude for God's involvement will confirm your faith and add energy to your Prayer. Once you have prayed, it is not necessary to continue to make the same request over and over again. Trust that God heard you the first time. Instead, pray and thank God for the answer to your Prayer.

As I have said before, the fall of 2005 was a challenging time for me. My house was still in shambles from Hurricane Charley and I had just fired my contractor, my husband, for his failure to timely make the necessary repairs. Divorce was imminent. My father was diagnosed with cancer and my mother had just recovered from a stroke.

I did not have the energy or resources to resolve these situations. I battled more fears than I had ever faced at one time. How would I finish the house and begin to live in a normal environment? Would my father survive cancer? I feared that chemotherapy and radiation would put him in a wheelchair because of his already weakened physical condition. Would my mother suffer another stroke as a result of all the stress? Statistics indicate cancer of the esophagus is difficult to conquer. They also indicate that after a person has suffered a stroke, they are more susceptible to a second one within the first year. I am grateful that God doesn't read the same statistics.

I turned it all over to God and spent my morning time in more Prayer and meditation. Every day began with my calling upon God for His blessings and protection. I prayed for the health and healing of my parents, for my health and well-being and for people to assist me in rebuilding the house. I prayed for my marriage and for protection from all the negative energies.

I thanked God for the health and healing of my parents and for my health and well-being. I thanked God for those people who were directed to me and assisted in the completion of the house. I thanked God for giving me direction in my marriage and for surrounding me with positive energies and His love.

In October 2006, I began planning a Thanksgiving celebration. It didn't just represent the November holiday. This occasion signified the culmination of the previous year's challenges and Prayers answered. The house was complete except for some small detail work. My mother's health was restored. My father was cancer-free and attended exercise classes for seniors at the gym. My divorce was final and I had found a sense of peace. When I realized how many blessings I had experienced in twelve months, I thanked God once again.

"There is nothing that wastes the body like worry, and one who has any faith in God should be ashamed to worry about anything whatsoever."
— *Mahatma Gandhi*

The *PowerShift* in Prayer is fully energized when you release the subject of your Prayer and turn it over to God completely. The practice of Prayer in faith allows you to release fear and let go of your worries and concerns. Worrying changes nothing. It's a habit to allow worrisome thoughts to pollute your mind and contaminate your mental processes. Worry steals your peace and robs you of joy. It inhibits your Prayer practice and prevents it from fully serving you.

There are times that I have the futile tendency to pray on a specific topic of concern only to find that moments later I am again worrying and trying to figure it out on my own. This process reminds me of the wind-up car children play with that goes forward until it hits an obstacle. The car then backs up and hits the same barrier over again. Unable to find an open space in which to proceed, the toy winds down by repeatedly hitting the same wall. The car must then be wound up again and placed in a different position. In much the same way, I have mulled over the same concern for which I have prayed. Like the car, I too, hit that wall repeatedly. Failing to locate an opening, I become exhausted and wind down. It is at this point that I quit worrying and turn it over to God in Prayer. Once God rewinds me, He places me in a more favorable position than I could find on my own.

It takes less energy to pray than to worry. Prayer also creates more positive energy. You do not have to figure everything out. When you are overloaded with the responsibilities of life, you block the good things from entering. Stop the worrying before it becomes pervasive in your mind. Once you have prayed over a matter, choose a scripture or affirmation that will support the object of your Prayer. As those thoughts and images of worry and anxiety develop in your mind, say the word cancel and immediately recite the scripture or affirmation that you have chosen. This will release the hold that the negative thoughts have on your mind, return the subject of your Prayer to God and allow Him to do His work.

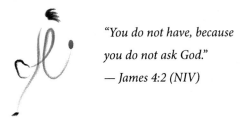

"You do not have, because you do not ask God."
— *James 4:2 (NIV)*

My Prayer practice has witnessed many blessings and miracles. My father, mother, friends and I have been healed by the *PowerShift* of Prayer. Medical intervention may have helped, but Divine intervention has been primarily responsible. During my time of Prayer, I had always asked for what

I needed and no more. I didn't want God to think I was selfish or asking for more than I deserved. With so many serious things occurring in the world, it seemed self-centered to ask for assistance with finances or a career. Was God really interested in my professional life? Did I really need to bother Him with the fact that I needed a new car or the money to pay my bills? In the middle of a Prayer a voice asked, "You have had the faith necessary for healings. Do you not think that I would do the same for your finances? Do you not think that you can ask me for the desires of your heart and that I will answer? Is your faith that limited?"

I contemplated those words: "Is your faith that limited?" My faith in God wasn't limited, however, my faith in myself was. I felt unworthy and believed I had to constantly prove myself before God and people in my life. My belief that I deserved to have life's best had been minimized. God delights in giving His blessings to those that call upon Him in love and faith. He is concerned about all aspects of life. My lack of faith in myself prevented me from fully enjoying all that God wanted to do for me.

"Pray in the Spirit at all times and on every occasion. Stay alert and be persistent in your prayers for all believers everywhere."
— *Ephesians 6:18 (NLT)*

"Is your faith that limited?" I began praying about everything: my needs and wants, the people for whom I should work, and about what was fair and equitable to charge my clients. My answers came from a Higher Source that possesses full knowledge of what is in my best interest. I now accept that I am worthy of the gifts, blessings and talents that I have been given, both tangible and intangible. I know that there is no need to worry about paying back. In God's eyes, all of my debts have already been paid. I am the child of a Loving Creator. I represent His love, abundance, joy and peace. To accept anything than the best that God has to offer will diminish me. To accept anything less than the best that my life has to offer is to diminish God.

"Again, I tell you that if two of you on earth agree about anything you ask for, it will be done for you by my Father in heaven. For where two or three come together in my name, there am I with them."
— *Matthew 18: 19-20 (NIV)*

Prayer has a feature that is unique among the *PowerShifts*. The other *PowerShifts* that you incorporate into your life are personal to you and are practiced individually in order to achieve optimal results. Prayer can be practiced both alone and collectively in a group. The power of Prayer is intensified when two or more people pray in agreement towards a common cause.

Shortly after my recovery from anorexia, my father became seriously ill. He was trying to overcome a sinus infection and had not been feeling well. One afternoon, he slipped into a coma. The paramedics were called and Dad was rushed to the hospital emergency room. A CAT scan was immediately performed and the results showed a dark mass on his brain. The neurologist on call determined that he probably wouldn't live through the hour. Surgery was inevitable if there was any hope of saving his life.

Miraculously, my father survived the surgery. The surgeons discovered a large infection covering his brain that was traced to his sinuses. As a result of the infection and the manner in which it had spread, my father was left with all the effects of a massive stroke. He remained in a coma in intensive care for four months, hooked up to respirators and various other pieces of medical equipment.

When you are in such a situation, you have no control over the outcome from an earthly perspective. The doctors, as talented, gifted and educated as they may be, are limited to their physical abilities. Prayer causes the supernatural to take place. My mother and I, as well as family and friends, prayed. My father was placed on Prayer lists at churches of friends, co-workers and acquaintances. There were hundreds of people praying in agreement for my father's recovery. Each time my mother and I walked into his room in intensive care we could feel the *PowerShift* of Prayer at work. It was as if there was an electrical charge being emitted. The medical equipment may have been monitoring my father's vital signs, yet there was also a powerful energy monitoring his vital life forces.

Weeks later, the doctors determined that my father would survive. They told us that his right side, however, would be paralyzed and he would never walk again. The extent of the other damage to his brain was yet unknown. There was more Prayer. Later that same day, my mother and I visited my father. Much to our delight, he wiggled his right toe.

Sixteen weeks after his admission to the emergency room, a man who had been given a medical death sentence was alive. Although he had been given a prognosis of paralysis, Dad walked. Each treating physician on the team acknowledged that his recovery was a miracle.

Another testimony to the *PowerShift* of Prayer in numbers and agreement occurred during my first year of law school. My mother became ill with the flu and the medication that the doctor prescribed caused her kidneys to shut down. Totally dehydrated, she was admitted to the hospital. Toxins backed up in her system and welts developed all over her body. Numerous tests were run. Mom was advised by the specialist that her kidneys were not functioning properly and she would be on dialysis for the rest of her life. Again, it would take the supernatural to restore my mother to health. She and I prayed in agreement for her full recovery.

The night before she was to start dialysis, my mother experienced a phenomenon within her body. She began passing urine and she became aware that her kidneys were being restored. In the morning, when the nurse came to take my mother to dialysis, my mother advised the attending technician that the procedure was no longer necessary. Tests were performed, once again, and confirmed what my mother already knew. The results proved that her kidneys were working and that she was no longer in need of dialysis. There was no medical explanation for the change in prognosis. Her recovery was attributed to a miracle. The return of function to her kidneys was an answer to our Prayers.

"When Job prayed for his friends, the Lord restored his fortunes. In fact, the Lord gave him twice as much as before!"
—*Job 42:10 (NLT)*

The internet is an exceptional tool for collective Prayer. Within hours, thousands of people can pray in agreement about a request being made. E-mails and websites allow you to access friends, on-line Prayer lists and groups with relative ease to unite in Prayer for a common cause. The power in this medium to create a positive force in Prayer is unlimited.

I have had the opportunity to witness this growing trend for Prayer partnerships. Melinda, a close friend, gave birth to Jake, a healthy baby boy. The joy of holding her newborn son in her arms was short-lived. Within a week after she brought him home, he became seriously ill. A trip to the doctor became an immediate admission to the local hospital. Tests indicated that Jake had contracted spinal meningitis. Without delay, he was transferred to another medical facility that was better equipped to handle his illness. The treating physicians advised Melinda that her son's minimum stay would be thirty days, if he survived at all. Assuming he lived, they further informed her that her son would be disabled.

My friend is a spiritual woman and knows the power of love and Prayer. She sent an e-mail to friends and family informing us of her son's illness and to ask for Prayer for his recovery. Her initial e-mails were forwarded to others requesting more Prayers. Jake's name was placed on Prayer lists throughout the internet and eventually was added to the Prayer lists of a multitude of congregations. Thousands of people were engaged to pray for this child's recovery.

When I spoke with Melinda, she commented that she felt the energy and power in the room, much like I had experienced in the hospital with my father. Her son was discharged from the hospital within two weeks of admittance. The staff of the medical facility placed a plaque with his name inscribed on the wall where they acknowledge their miracles. Today, he is a normal child leading a full life with minimal lasting effects from his life-threatening illness. Jake's story serves as a daily reminder of a miracle invoked by the Prayers of thousands praying in agreement.

"I have had prayers answered – most strangely so sometimes –but I think our heavenly Father's loving –kindness has been even more evident in what he has refused me."
— *Lewis Carroll*

Does God answer every Prayer? There may be times when you pray and your outcome is not what you wanted or the answer is not within your time frame. In Prayer, you must relinquish the absolute control to God. You must trust His higher judgment and be satisfied with His answer. Perhaps the correct question that you should ask yourself is, If you pray for a solution and don't get the answer the way that you want it, do you want a solution or do you want control?

There are countless times where I have been thankful that my Prayers weren't answered in the manner or time frame that I requested. I have learned to trust God to know what is in my highest good. I know He always acts in my best interest. His discernment is more accurate than mine and His perspective is greater than mine.

As I said earlier, in the summer of 1992 I worked in Fort Myers, a city on the west coast of Florida. I took my two horses with me and boarded them at a private facility owned by a caring, responsible woman. Plans changed, as they often do, and I returned to Miami during the first week of August. I could not find anyone to haul my horses back to the east coast and they remained three hours away from me. I prayed that God would help me find someone. No one showed up. I became frustrated over the delay. Three weeks later on August 24, 1992, Hurricane

Andrew made landfall in South Dade. The furious winds and waters left no evidence of the barn that would have stabled my horses had my Prayers been answered within my time frame. They wouldn't have had a chance of survival. God's delays and detours are not necessarily God's denials. Sometimes, they are God's deliverance.

Immediately following the storm, I went out to view the devastation. Everything had been destroyed. Most of the trees were uprooted and tossed like toothpicks. There were piles of concrete blocks where buildings once stood. In the midst of the rubble, I saw a pay phone that remained standing. No one else had noticed it. I made my way over to it and picked up the receiver. There was a dial tone. I immediately called the woman who was caring for my horses in Fort Myers. I had no idea where the storm had gone after it left South Dade, but I knew that the facility where my horses were staying could have been directly in its terrorizing path.

The woman answered the phone and sounded thankful to hear my voice. Throughout the night, she and her husband had watched the storm's ravaging effects on television. They prayed for my family's survival. Fort Myers had been spared and she assured me that my horses were okay. Other people, who were wandering in shock, saw me on the phone and began to form a line. After our two minute conversation, I hung up in order to allow others to make calls. Suddenly, there was no more dial tone. The phone was totally dead. I had been able to make the only call.

The months following Hurricane Andrew were difficult. Knowing my horses had survived the tragic event made getting through each day bearable. God did hear my Prayers and He knew what was in my best interest. My Prayers were answered but in His time. He had spared my horses. Six months later, they returned safely home.

There are also times when another's Prayers may supersede yours. When anorexia had a stronghold on me, depression and exhaustion dominated my will to live. I prayed for God to take me. I awoke each morning wondering why I was still alive. My mother did everything possible to save me. She made appointments with therapists to deal with my mental and emotional state, took me to doctors for my physical well-being and she had hired a nutritionist to help me eat properly again. Nothing worked. My physical and mental health continued to deteriorate.

My mother did everything possible to prevent me from harming myself further. She also prayed. She prayed for God's help to direct her path in my recovery, for the restoration of my health and well-being and that I would not succumb to this disorder that had control over my mind and body.

Her strong love and faith created an environment for God to intervene. Her Prayers prevailed over mine and I fully recovered from anorexia. My health was restored physically, mentally and spiritually. I am grateful that God listened to my Prayers and, knowing my heart, chose to act in my highest interest in His response. I am thankful that He listened to the Prayers of a loving, devoted mother and answered her petition instead of mine.

"Come to me, all of you who are weary and carry heavy burdens, and I will give you rest."
— *Matthew 11:28 (NLT)*

When the heart is heavy, the soul cannot grow. Prayer releases the heaviness and weight that you carry in the physical world. Your fears are dissipated and the burdens of your responsibilities are discharged. Prayer allows you to do what you can do and God does the rest. In Prayer, your mind and spirit become rejuvenated and open to accepting all the positive possibilities that this divine universe offers. From this position, you achieve your goals and manifest your dreams. From this place, you forgive and are forgiven. In this energy, you overcome conflicts and challenges. It is here that you enter into an enduring state of gratitude. From this place, you are free to live your purpose, master your goals, manifest your dreams and create a *PowerShift*!

PowerShift Reflection - In His rest, you connect to the Divine and come to know God. In Prayer, you enter into a state of peace mentally, physically and spiritually. You know that all is well. This is God's Grace and your point of true power. This is the place where all of the PowerShifts gain momentum. As the righteousness of God and a child of the Creator, you have a right to stand boldly in His presence and receive all of the answers that you need.

CHAPTER
FIVE

POWERSHIFT: DIVINE DIRECTION

"And the Lord said to them, "Now listen to what I say: "If there were prophets among you, I, the Lord, would reveal myself in visions. I would speak to them in dreams."

— *Numbers 12:6 (NLT)*

The *PowerShift* of Prayer is our way of getting in touch with the Divine and communicating with God. So how does God communicate with us? There are moments, dreams, interactions with other people or things, or a simple word or act that occur in daily life that may seemingly be of little importance. However, they are God's way of shifting you in purpose or supporting you through transitions or adversity. The contact may be subtle or it may be quite significant. You may not even be immediately aware of the effects. The shift, however, continues to disseminate into your mental and spiritual being until there is a moment of enlightenment. Visualize a pebble dropped into the water, its ripples emanating outward long after the stone has drifted to the bottom. Similarly, God's Divine Direction radiates its effect throughout your entire life from a single moment in time and continues the *PowerShift*.

*"Whenever you have truth, it must be given with love
or the message and the messenger will be rejected."*
— *Mahatma Gandhi*

The messages conveyed through interactions with those around us may appear to depend on the specific situation in which they evolved. The meaning of the messages in our lives, however, comes to light as we hear that voice in our head repeating them during subsequent situations. The impact of their words is the same whether they are long-term friends or mere acquaintances. It is not the medium; it is the message that is significant.

In my first years in real estate sales, I worked for an office manager that I greatly admired. She had the gift of motivating people and, although everyone in our office had personal challenges of their own, her professionalism and enthusiasm formed us into a successful sales team.

There was a time that I was involved with a transaction that wouldn't go smoothly no matter what I did. Every time a closing date was set something went wrong and I had to start from the beginning. The transaction was not significant from a monetary standpoint and it drained much of my time and energy. It also prevented me from being more productive with other clients. This transaction became more than a challenge or a business deal. I was determined to see it through on principle alone.

One day, in the midst of my frustration, my manager approached me and simply said, "Let it go." This phrase was a simple directive; however, it was difficult for me to act upon and embrace. At that stage of my life, letting go meant admitting defeat. I took it as a blow to my abilities and my ego. However, when I finally did release the transaction, I also relinquished the pressure and negative energy preventing me from moving forward. Ironically, when I let it go, the deal came together and closed.

"Let it go" has echoed in my mind from that day forward. The meaning implied in that basic statement was, "You are holding on to this for all of the wrong reasons and they are not worth your time and energy." Often, when we attempt to force an outcome, we block the positive energy.

Even today, I hear these words whenever I become entrenched in a business transaction or personal matter where a resolution turns into a struggle. This powerful phrase continues to provide me with a tool to release pressure and negative energy in these situations. It also allows me to re-examine my personal motivation and reaffirm my objectivity in the matter. Once my intentions are realigned, I know that whatever the outcome, it will be in the highest and best good for all involved.

"Kind words can be short and easy to speak, but their echoes are truly endless."
— *Mother Teresa*

There is another *PowerShift* phrase that is personal to me. The words are, "It doesn't matter." In my early twenties I had a riding instructor that believed in teaching through positive statements and encouragement. I only had the opportunity to ride with him a short time, but those lessons have since had a direct impact on my life. He wanted his students to use the power of the mind to benefit their riding abilities, rather than to criticize themselves and inhibit their skills and talents. He believed that whatever you focused on in your riding, you received. Therefore, if you were not doing something correctly on a horse and tried to do it right, the pressure of the correction would cause you to overcompensate. Your mind would be obsessed on the fact that you were doing it wrong.

During my training, if there was something that I wasn't doing properly, he briefly brought it to my attention. He guided me on what I should feel and gave me suggestions on how to correct it. His comments were always completed with the phrase, "It doesn't matter." Then, he immediately re-directed my focus to something that I was doing right.

If I thought I had not performed well or struggled with a movement, my muscles would tighten and my breathing would become shallow. Anyone who has ever ridden a horse, or engaged in any sport, knows it is impossible to function athletically with constricted muscles and while holding your breath! "It doesn't matter," however, prevented me from becoming stressed and rigid and allowed me to get out of my own way. Almost effortlessly, the improper technique or position corrected itself without exerting a great deal of energy.

The phrase, "It doesn't matter," has gone beyond my love of horseback riding and continues to influence my thought process in every area of my life. My trainer coached excellent horses and riders to top honors and always maintained his theory that if you aren't having fun, you have no business being there. If I experience significant stress or anxiety or if I am confronted with a challenging situation, his words and theory return to my mind as I recall the lessons once more.

Often, we lose our effectiveness and joy and sabotage our talents through a continuous stream of self-criticism and judgment. If we don't choke under the pressure, at the very least we disrupt our physical health. We take the joy out of our lives with the constant barrage of brain-babble telling us that we are not good enough or we could have done better. Three words, once again, allow me to shift my mindset from my own mental attack and restore a sense of peace and pleasure in my life.

Phrases such as "let it go" or "it doesn't matter" are said to or by us daily. What makes words such as these a *PowerShift*? Although the context or the situation in which they were spoken gives them the relevance and definition in your life, they evolve from a higher level and are designed to be a tool for your own private use. Their meaning becomes personal and subliminally resonates deep within your inner being. The power within the message may subtly exert its influence, but it can always be accessed by you at anytime when needed.

"All God's angels come to us disguised."
— *James Russell Lowell*

A *PowerShift* message can also come through your interaction with different things. Whenever you become engaged in the energy of another being that interrupts a negative mental mindset and directs your energy and thought process on a more positive path, you have experienced a *PowerShift*. You may not realize the shift in power from the interaction immediately, but the meaning and benefits of the message will become apparent in time.

One April morning, as the crispness of spring touched the air, I jogged around my neighborhood. During the course of my journey, I discussed with God the numerous worries that were creating my stress and anxiety. I can't say it was a conversation because I was doing all of the talking.

In the middle of my manic meditation, I passed my neighbor's son, who was waiting for his school bus. He yelled to me, "Do you want a cat?" The question took me by surprise. He was not holding a cat. In his hands was a two-week-old kitten. The school bus was approaching fast so I took the kitten from the young man and headed towards my house. As I walked home sobbing, I realized that her mother was a feral cat that roamed my neighborhood. The kitten had similar colors and markings. More than likely, something interrupted the mother cat while moving her litter, forcing her to leave this little one behind.

Suddenly, on top of everything else, I now had a two-week-old kitten relying on me for its survival. As I walked into the house both the kitten and I were crying. What part of the conversation did God not understand? Stress reduction does not include added responsibility.

The weeks that followed were focused on Zoe. Acting as a surrogate mother became a second full-time job. Feeding and playing with her were time-consuming, but every moment with her was a joy. Her presence had a magical energy. Without realizing it, my energy shifted away from my other worries and focused on this little fur ball of unconditional love.

Six weeks later, Zoe was a healthy black and white kitten with magnificent markings. On her black back was a flawless white heart. Incredibly, all those issues that had consumed my energies resolved themselves without further worry or concern on my part. This cherished, God-given angel had shifted my power. It was one of those moments where God doesn't give you what you want but He gives you what you need.

I forgot to engage the tools and strategies that I know to use when life becomes overridden with pressures and anxieties. Instead, I gave God a laundry list of things that needed to be changed or fixed. I needed a *PowerShift* and Zoe's presence was the catalyst for that shift. There was nothing constructive in my manner of thinking. My attention had been directed to lack, fear, and a host of other negative influences. My thoughts blocked the positive energy and I was immobilized from taking any definite actions.

When Zoe entered my life, my energy shifted to Love. This, alone, removed the challenges that I experienced. The vibration of the energy around me began to improve. In holding this magnificent little angel, my thoughts shifted from apprehension and fear to life and love. In playing with her, my tears shifted to laughter. There is no greater power to shift the energy and transform your life than the power of Love. There is truth in the quote by Emmett Fox, "If only you could love enough, you would be the most powerful person in the world."

"*The golden moments in the stream of life rush past us and we see nothing but sand; the angels come to visit us, and we only know them when they are gone.*"
— *George Eliot*

There are messages and messengers of Love walking among us each day. They can be anyone, at anytime. Each encounter, no matter how brief, will touch your soul. They meet our hidden needs and heal the hidden hurts that we keep deep within our hearts. They are our own personal fan club cheering on our human spirit, extending open arms when we need consoling. Their very presence reminds us that there is a Higher Power, that there is a God. Their Divine expressions of Love may be simple gestures or heroic efforts. Their Divine communications may be kind words or verbal warnings. The key is to learn to recognize them and remain receptive to their messages and actions.

One evening on a particularly hurried day, I rushed to pick up a take-out order for dinner. I parked the car and hurried to the carry-out window to retrieve my food. As I approached, I noticed a cherubic-looking man sitting on the bench in the waiting area. He was heavy-set with a warm smile and a twinkle in his eye. He caught my attention because he wore an ascot, a hat that you don't often see in South Florida. As we made eye contact, he said, "Honey, slow down." I nodded, smiled and paid for my order. When I turned to leave, he was gone. I looked for him in both the waiting area and parking lot. There was no sign of him anywhere.

I have no doubt that he was an angel who crossed my life's path. It wasn't a life-threatening moment. I was not in danger. I was rushing around lost in thought, failing to experience each minute for the Divine joy that is within it. That momentous meeting was a *PowerShift* that reinforced that my life is gift. Each moment is God-given and is meant to be enjoyed.

"*Do not neglect to show hospitality to strangers, for by doing that some have entertained angels without knowing it.*"
— *Hebrews 13:2(NIV)*

A similar experience occurred during a business trip. I had to catch an early morning flight home and head directly into a meeting at my office upon my return. I left the hotel dressed in business attire with my make-up case and overnight bag on my shoulder. The sun had not yet come up and I boarded a public transportation system that should have taken me to the airport.

Suddenly, I had an uncomfortable feeling that my train was heading in the wrong direction. The hotel concierge had given me directions and told me which train would take me to my destination. It was still dark as I looked out the windows and I couldn't see where I was or what was around me. Fearing I would miss my flight, I got off at the next stop to get my bearings.

Yes, I discovered I had been traveling in the wrong direction! However, exiting alone in the predawn hours in an unfamiliar major city was not one of my best decisions. I was in a high-crime area surrounded by an unsavory group of men. It was still dark as the train pulled out and I stood on the platform wearing a suit and high heels trying not to look obvious.

The look didn't work and a dozen pair of eyes stared at me. A man who had been off to himself approached. The tension increased with each step he took towards me and my fight or flight system kicked into gear. He stood in front of me smiling and said, "Honey, you're lost." I sighed with relief and let out a nervous laugh. I found myself at the mercy of a stranger who came out of nowhere. He remained by my side until the next train pulled in, then boarded with me and rode to the station where my connecting train waited. He then escorted me onto the platform to the train which would take me to the airport. Thanking him graciously, we said goodbye and parted ways.

I made my flight and my meeting that day. More important than that, however, was the Divine connection I experienced in the train station. In that moment where I was lost and anxious, I was reminded that angels and messengers walk among us. They guide and protect us. When we acknowledge their presence and the message they leave, a *PowerShift* is created affirming that we have access to love and protection.

"When it was time to leave, they returned to their own country by another route, for God had warned them in a dream not to return to Herod."
— *Matthew 2:12 (NLT)*

PowerShift messages can come to us through our dreams because we are open to accepting the presence of the messenger and more receptive to the communication of the message itself. During a dream state, our attention may be directed to an answer for which we are searching or a moral to a lesson we need to learn. There are also dreams where we are directed to pay attention to a warning that may advise us of a threat or danger. Drastic measures may be used to invade our awareness and jog our memory when we awaken.

Typically, the *PowerShift* and reoccurring theme in the messages, no matter their purpose, is the overwhelming presence of love. I have previously shared how I recovered from anorexia as the direct result of Divine intervention that came in the form of a dream. The dream was vivid and the message was strong. There was an awe-inspiring presence of love. This presence is the defining point I use to distinguish dreams containing messages from those which are merely a culmination of my subconscious thoughts.

Another dream that served as Divine Direction in my life came during a period where I suffocated my gifts and talents. I became stuck and couldn't move forward or step into my purpose as a result of my own fears. In this dream, I was guided to a fish which struggled to breathe in shallow waters. His body flipped, and with each movement of his gills, he searched for the sustenance of his life. Once again, a Loving Being appeared.

Coming with a message, she pointed to the fish and instructed me to pick it up and place it in deeper waters. I did as she directed. Once free to swim in open waters, the fish revived and developed into a much larger, thriving fish. My dream came to an end as I watched him soar through the air and plunge, with his natural power and force, into the water below.

In the morning when I awoke, I knew that this had been a spiritual communication containing a powerful message. Although I had a good understanding of the meaning, during a meditation, I asked for the translation of this dream. When attempting to determine the meaning of a message, it is to your advantage to go within and put the pieces together in the context of your own life. The message was given to you and you must be the one to understand its meaning. There are sources in the physical world that you can call on to interpret it for you. However, the substance of the communication must be one that resonates within your own being. In other words, heed the message but beware of the interpretation.

The answer to my question in my meditation was not complicated. I, like the fish, was suffocating in the shallow water. I was in a period of my life where I allowed my personal fears to hinder my growth and development. I needed to get out of my own way, take a leap of faith and swim in the deep open waters. In doing so, I would thrive and grow.

I have had other dreams that have placed me in situations where I am struggling or am not physically able to do what needs to be done. Inevitably, at the right moment, I hear the message, "Use your mind." Heeding that, I call on the energy of my thoughts and am able to liberate myself or perform whatever task is necessary. These types of dreams usually occur during my inner struggles when I lose my peace and joy in the situation. During these periods, I usually become so rooted in trying to free myself with external sources that I neglect to empower myself by fully summoning the resources of my mental and spiritual skills. This type of gentle reminder gets me back in purpose and the message serves as a *PowerShift* in my life.

"He will order his angels to protect and guard you.
And they will hold you up with their hands
so you won't even hurt your foot on a stone."
— Luke 4:10-11 (NLT)

There are also *PowerShift* messages that direct and demand nothing less than immediate attention and obedience. I am certain you have heard stories where a person would have experienced severe bodily injury or death if they had not received supernatural intervention. There is no place or time for the human thought process when one of these messages is conveyed.

One day I was driving on a major interstate that had eight lanes of traffic. The highway was divided by a concrete median into four lanes in each direction. As I listened to music and thought of my last meeting, a spirit voice directed me, 'Get over.' Without thinking, I complied with the instructions. This action placed my car in the inside lane, directly next to the concrete barricade in the median. I am not comfortable driving next to concrete barriers and seldom end up in this lane. Seconds earlier, a car had passed me in the inside lane and when I moved over it was directly in front of me.

Ahead of us sat a disabled vehicle on the shoulder adjacent to the median. The car in front of me appeared to have clipped the disabled car as it passed. The driver lost control of the car and turned toward the barricade. Attempting to avoid one collision, he jerked the vehicle sharply back onto the highway and crossed four lanes of traffic diagonally at a high rate of speed. The events that followed appeared to be in slow motion and almost surreal in nature. The driver involved six more cars in this accident and others frantically attempted to navigate through the chaos.

My obedience to the voice allowed me to steer through the danger unharmed. I was shaken up by what I witnessed and more so when I realized the importance of the message I had received. By driving in the lane near the barricade, my vehicle was positioned to avoid the danger. If the car in front of me had hit the disabled vehicle and struck the wall when it turned toward the median, I would have been unable to slow my speed in time to stop my car and avoid a deadly collision. Or, if I had not listened to the voice and changed lanes, I would have been involved in the accident in another way. My car would have been one of the automobiles that collided with the out-of-control car as it sped across the highway to the opposite shoulder.

On another occasion, I was exiting off the ramp from the same highway. The exit was designed to direct the cars to an overpass. A stop light intersected the ramp and the overpass. At this point, I had the red light and was first in line to accelerate when the light changed.

Repairs were being performed on the overpass and changes were being made to the lanes. Large barricades and a construction trailer parked in one of the closed lanes blocked my sight. I was unable to see any traffic to my left as the cars proceeded into the intersection. I was totally dependent upon the traffic signal for direction.

The light turned green and I took my foot off the brake. The same voice that had protected me before spoke again. As my foot touched the gas pedal, I heard the word, "Stop!" I was startled and immediately slammed on the brakes. At that moment, a loaded eighteen-wheeler barreled through the red light. He had failed to slow his rig as he approached the signal. When the light changed, he had no option but to speed through the intersection. Considering his rig's rate of speed and size, had I not listened to the voice and acted accordingly, the driver's side of my car would have been struck with such force that the impact would have pushed it across the overpass.

I share these stories to emphasize the importance of being open to the communication and messages that are part of everyday life. They are lessons that will be forever embedded in your memory and have the ability to positively and powerfully influence your thought processes and actions. They will be there when you confront challenges and face adversity. They will be there to direct you in purpose and to the pathway of mastering your goals and manifesting your dreams. They will be there to remind you that you are loved. These messages of love, guidance and protection create a God-given *PowerShift* in your life.

"We can all be angels to one another. We can choose to obey the still small stirring within, the little whisper that says, 'Go. Ask. Reach out. Be an answer to some one's plea. You have a part to play. Have faith.' We can decide to risk that He is indeed there, watching, caring, cherishing us as we love and accept love. The world will be a better place for it. And wherever they are, the angels will dance."
—Joan Wester Anderson

There are also times when you become the messenger and create the *PowerShift* in the lives of others. A stirring in your soul or a whisper in your mind may encourage you to speak or perform some deed for another. It may be to brighten someone's day or to act as the catalyst for necessary change in someone's life. You may never know the outcome of your words or actions. Your purpose is solely to communicate that which is needed or to act upon a certain situation when guided to do so. Anything more lies in the heart of the recipient and in the hands of a loving Higher Power.

Early in my legal practice, I settled a case and was delivering some papers to opposing counsel for signature. We finished our business and the conversation turned casual. There were pictures of his grown daughters on his desk and I politely inquired about them. He was a proud father and shared how he missed spending time with his girls. Thinking they may be living out of town, I asked why he had not seen them. He responded that managing the office and practicing law took too many hours out of his week. His work prevented him from spending the leisure time with his daughters that he once did.

The discussion had been light up until this point in our conversation. The next words that I spoke, however, took me by surprise. I didn't have time to think about or process what I said or the manner in which I said it. I told him that he needed to take the time to be with his daughters. He needed to make the effort to share the lives of the people who loved him. I also said that if anything happened to him, the only office calls that his clients would make would be to locate their files and make arrangements for their transfer. Somewhat shocked, he nodded in agreement. Our conversation ended and I left his office.

I never had the opportunity to work with him again, nor did we have any further contact. Six months later, however, I saw his picture in the newspaper. It was above his obituary. I knew that the words I spoke that day were meant to impact his life and create a *PowerShift*. However, I never knew whether they motivated him to act. I never learned whether he had the opportunity to spend the much-needed time with his daughters prior to his untimely passing. It was not for me to know. I was only the instrument for the message.

His passing was not the end of the influence of the words that were spoken that day. Years later, after Hurricane Charley, I found myself constantly fatigued. I felt the stress and strain of practicing law and simultaneously dealing with life's personal challenges. I took a vacation get-away to the mountains to rest, relax and recharge. However, I also took my notebook computer because of a pending business transaction.

Clients called me with urgent situations during my time-off. I reviewed documents and read my e-mail. I discussed legal matters on my cell phone as I walked the streets of the quaint small town that was supposed to be my source of solitude and solace.

When I returned from my trip, I tied up all pending matters. Since the holidays were approaching, I closed my office until after the New Year in an effort to restore my sense of physical health and well-being.

I shared with you the events that surrounded Hurricane Charley: my marriage immediately prior to the storm, the category-four hurricane, the subsequent 24 months of repairs to the house, the death of my horse, my mother's stroke, my father's diagnosis with cancer and an inoperable aneurysm and my subsequent divorce. In spite of what happened in my personal life, I still had clients that needed my professional services. Thankfully, during the holiday season, the house was almost completely restored, my parents were doing well and business was slow.

I rarely experience an emergency or crisis in my practice of law. However, during these weeks off I repeatedly received calls that began with, "I need you to…," or "I know you are on a break but could you…," or "You gotta…" With every call, I felt my energy draining. Often times when people want their own needs met, they may unconsciously cross boundaries to get what they desire. It is our responsibility to know our boundaries and limitations and to insure that those lines are respected for our own physical, mental and spiritual well-being. I failed to do that. I did not take time to meet my own needs. I did not take time to honor myself or maintain my joy. I was no longer in charge of my life. I gave up my power and lived from one person's needs to another.

During prayer and meditation, I asked how to regain my power and shift this energy that controlled my life. The words I spoke to my opposing counsel fifteen years earlier came into my mind. I recalled his weariness and overall fatigue. He had lost the balance in his life and was overwhelmed. I remembered the things that he wanted to do, but continued to allow his work to be the sole determining factor in his life. He had lost his joy. Seeing myself in the same place, I now had the opportunity to restore mine.

The remaining time that I took was spent reflecting, reprioritizing and restructuring my life. There were personal and professional projects I wanted to complete. There was a path that I had postponed following. There was a purpose for which I had been preparing. It was now time to implement all those things that I had been deferring to another time. My own words, the message that I had given years earlier, created a *PowerShift* in my life.

"*Intuition will tell the thinking mind where to look next.*"
— *Jonas Salk*

Divine Direction is present each day of our lives. The Direction guides you in your purpose and in mastering your goals and manifesting your dreams. The fortuitous meetings, the dreams and visions, the still small voice that you hear in your head are all forms of Divine Guidance. As these messages become embedded in our beings, they strengthen our connection to the Divine Director and create a *PowerShift*!

PowerShift Reflection – Divine Direction guides, protects, assists in our growth and lets us know that we are loved. We can hear the messages in times of danger and adversity or within the silence of our souls. We can use them to propel us to the path of our purpose or hold them within our spirit when we need strength. The messages can be given by a person we know or a stranger we meet on the streets. They can invade our dreams, subtly enter our hearts or insistently enter our minds. They can encourage us to be the messenger for another and, in a turn of events, be the message we need to hear for ourselves.

CHAPTER
SIX

POWERSHIFT: TIME AND FOCUS

"Time is the coin of your life. It is the only coin you have, and only you can determine how it will be spent. Be careful lest you let other people spend it for you."
— Carl Sandburg

You must make the most of your valuable resources when you are confronted with life's challenges and in the midst of adversity, or living in purpose and mastering your goals, Time and Focus are tools that are of critical importance when managing challenges, adversity and transitions. Your ability to properly utilize them also impacts growth in the direction of your purpose, the mastery of your goals and the manifestation of your dreams. They establish your priorities and appropriately manage and master the moments in your day. Together, Time and Focus serve as a life- management system that will allow you to create your future in advance and support your dreams, goals and purpose.

Time is more than counting the seconds in each minute, the minutes in each hour and the hours in each day. Time is a resource that can never be stored or held in reserve. Once used, it can never be regained. Think of Time as the currency of your life. Whatever you choose to spend this currency on must be worth the exchange rate. Therefore, Time, like any investment, must be managed prudently. Defining your priorities takes this precious commodity and encourages you to allocate it to that which will produce the greater good for your life.

Focus is the process of maintaining your energy and power totally in the present moment on your priorities. The present moment is your point of power. It is difficult to live a purpose-filled life if you allow yourself to be manipulated by too many external influences. Focus is the internal discipline that allows the momentum to continue in the proper course when everything around you seems to be pulling you in other directions. It is the shift that places the full force of your mind into the concentration of a specific area and sustains your energy and inner power fully in the present and on purpose.

Taking authority over your Time and controlling your Focus is essential to dealing with adversity or averting it altogether. Ironically, many of our challenges can be created by our inability to focus on the task at hand or to use our time efficiently and judiciously. Taking dominion over your opportunities and activities each moment also creates a flow towards your goals and dreams to live a life of purpose. Focusing on that which you desire, prioritizing your actions and allotting the appropriate Time, and managing interferences create the *PowerShift*.

"*In his heart a man plans his course, but the LORD determines his steps.*"
— *Proverbs 16:9 (NIV)*

Moving into your purpose with success and significance or over-coming challenges and adversity requires a simple equation:

Ability + Action - Interruptions = Accomplishment

Ask yourself, "What purpose will this action serve my goal or outcome?" Time and Focus are the variables in this equation which will assist you in getting the correct answer. Establishing your priorities sets a cause in motion. Objectives become clear and the number of interferences becomes significantly reduced. Your life is defined by determining what will take precedence during your day, week, month and year. Your life is designed by maintaining the power of your concentration into your purpose, goals and dreams. Today's priorities will produce the life that you are living tomorrow.

"There is a time for everything, and a season for every activity under heaven."

— *Ecclesiastes 3:1 (NIV)*

Life management is based on the question, "What do I need to do today that is in alignment with my dreams, goals and purpose?" It is well-known that 20% of your actions generate 80% of your results. Take the responsibility to manage yourself. Concentrate on controlling what you can control: you and your environment

We search endlessly among the highly publicized production of day planners, PDAs (personal digital assistants) and other hi-tech toys to find an extra hour in the day to complete our to do list. This list may leave you wondering what you have truly accomplished. You may have crossed out the majority of the items, but still feel unfulfilled. Involving yourself in excessive amounts of busy work to prove to the rest of the world that you are accomplishing something will only exhaust you. The levels of success that you seek to achieve will only continue to elude you.

I use a legal pad and a day planner because I enjoy crossing items off. I don't experience the same level of accomplishment by deleting something off a computer screen. Often, though, for every item I cross off, I add two more. Unless I consciously review my activities and consider how they support my goals and dreams, I find myself exhausted with only an empty cardboard shell from a legal pad to show for my efforts. It is a false sense of accomplishment.

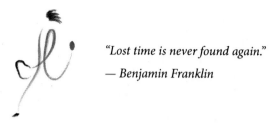

"Lost time is never found again."
— Benjamin Franklin

If you fail to establish priorities and create a structure to maintain their hierarchy of significance, you leave yourself vulnerable to disruptions and distractions that continually draw you off course. The events I describe are not the major life events such as a serious illness, accident or natural disaster. Major life events such as these require their own navigating. The events with which I am concerned in this section are those that rob you of your Time and Focus, drain your energy, distract you from your goals and dreams, and may divert you off purpose.

LIEs: Life-Interrupting Events

Daily detours may seem minor; however, their strength is in their innocent appeal and in the number of times they can seduce you away from your goals. At the end of the day you have been possessed by distractions and diversions which have depleted your energy and stolen the Time you planned to dedicate to your dreams. You LIE to yourself that you have accomplished something, although you are not sure exactly what. Take inventory of the day's activities or thought processes and you will know the LIEs. These are LIEs that you tell yourself to rationalize those things, events or people that took your energy and power, and left you no further along on your chosen path. They are Life- Interrupting Events. You LIE to yourself that you have good reasons for failing to accomplish that which you set out to do. Your explanations fall short because your soul and spirit know the truth.

There are three primary types of LIEs. Each LIE is detrimental to overcoming challenges and is lethal to your goals and dreams. The first two LIEs are Stress, and Demands and Expectations. These LIEs are embedded in external events and their energy originates from other people and things. The third LIE is Instant Gratification. This LIE finds its strength within our own minds and encourages us to avoid our priorities.

Permitted to linger long enough, each LIE can become pervasive and poisonous to your purpose. In order to live the life that you envision, you must be able to recognize whether you are an active or passive participant in the LIE. Once you become aware of your contribution to the process, shift your focus back to the truth. The truth is always defined by your purpose and those actions, thoughts and events that will direct you to the fulfillment of your goals and dreams.

LIE #1 - Stress

"Nothing is more effective than a deep, slow inhale and release for surrendering what you can't control and focusing again on what is right in front of you."
— *Oprah Winfrey*

THREE LIES

• STRESS

• DEMANDS & EXPECTATION

• INSTANT GRATIFICATION

The first LIE that we tell ourselves occurs when we become preoccupied with any thing, person or event that causes stress and anxiety. Our focus is shifted to past, present or future matters over which we have little or no control. It is easy to get caught up in the crisis of the moment or the daily dilemma. Our attention is either diverted to the matter at hand or we find ourselves distracted and triggered by things which occurred in the past that we have not released or fear will happen in the future.

When we allow the stress to direct our lives long enough, we become fueled by the adrenaline and addicted to the rush. We may even subconsciously seek out the next crisis or stress-inducing event to get our fix. It takes a proactive position to deliberately extricate ourselves from this addiction and maintain focus. If, instead, we take a reactive posture, acting hastily without thinking things through, it will only drain our mental and physical faculties. The resulting outcome will be chaos and confusion, more stress and additional anxiety. At the end of the day, we know we have been busy and that we are tired. We also know we have made little to no progress on purpose and in the direction of our goals and dreams.

This is not to say that all stress-inducing moments fall into the category of the first LIE. There are those pressure-pumped matters that require our Time and Focus. The first LIE involves those things which, if we stepped back and looked at our participation from an objective standpoint, we would find that our involvement was totally unnecessary. The first LIE is the Time and Focus that you give to the ridiculous fight that you had with your spouse or significant other. You may continue to play it over and over in your mind only to become angrier and more hurt. The first LIE is the anxiety you have over a low bank account. The stress that you experience knowing that you cannot pay your bills only robs you of the Time and Focus to manifest the funds you need. No matter how many times you check your bank account, the numbers work out the same. You may become anxious and focused on how to cover one check and you lose the opportunity to make much more.

The key to extricating yourself from the first LIE is awareness. Take a deep breath, relax for a moment and remove yourself from the emotion of the situation. Ask yourself, "Is my involvement or attention to this matter truly necessary and productive?" If the answer is no, by taking this moment of reflection you become aware of your participation in the LIE. From this point of consciousness you can choose to remove yourself from the situation.

If, on the other hand, the answer is yes, your next question would be, "Is my involvement or attention to this matter necessary and productive to this extent?" If the answer is no, then you have the ability to reduce the amount of Time and Focus you are giving to the situation and bring it into alignment. If the answer to this question is yes, then your involvement is required and you are not participating in a LIE.

While I was writing this chapter, my father suffered a stroke. The previous damage to his brain was located on the left side. The effects of this event occurred on the right side of my father's brain. My days became filled with conversations with numerous doctors whose opinions differed from one another. There was also a constant dialog with the nurses who were in charge of him. This was a life and death matter and major life decisions had to be made almost daily. Friends and other family members who were genuinely concerned for my father's well-being called to get status reports on his condition. Each day's activities left me exhausted by evening. A week quickly passed and I had not written or made any further progress on the book. My dream, my goal, had been set aside. I wasn't motivated or inspired. My father required my Time and Focus.

During the second week of his hospital stay, my father stabilized. He was placed on a feeding tube and catheter and it appeared he would survive. He could move his left side but his speech was incomprehensible. My mind became preoccupied with questions. Would my father still be able to walk and move on his own? If not, how would we manage him when he was released? Would his speech return? Would he be able to indicate his needs? He recognized people but where was he in his own brain? How would this affect his personality? Would he be able to eat again or would he have to continue the feeding tube? If he could eat, would he be able to feed himself? My anxious brain searched for answers and found none.

There would be none for the next few months. Before he could return home, my father would undergo weeks of occupational, physical and speech therapy in a rehabilitation unit. The resulting effects of my father's stroke and how to rearrange life in order to accommodate his needs remained unknown. This stressful process of attempting to predict the future soon wore me out. Days turned into weeks, and I had accomplished nothing towards my purpose. Then I received that spiritual tap on the shoulder reminding me that my Focus on an outcome over which I had no immediate control was not required. My Focus was now being consumed by a LIE.

The following week, my father was transferred from the hospital to the nursing home where his days were now scheduled with activities to engage and rehabilitate his brain and body. Qualified therapists worked with him, stimulating his mental and physical processes. My presence was not as necessary and my visits shortened. My life returned to a modified level of normalcy. I began to schedule select clients in my practice and took an hour to work out at the gym or take a walk in the neighborhood. I also began to write again. My modified schedule allowed me to return to my goals and dreams, while spending the necessary Time and Focus on my father.

LIE #2 – Demands and Expectations

"Let your eyes look straight ahead, fix your gaze directly before you."
—*Proverbs 4:25 (NIV)*

The second LIE that deprives us of giving necessary attention to our purpose is the demands of others. This is not to say that other's needs should not be a part of our priorities. On the contrary, as a parent, spouse, employer or employee we all have people in our lives whose needs are a priority. It is the continuous attempt to meet everyone's needs, desires and requirements at every moment that steals your time, robs you of your focus and depletes your energy. If you constantly try to do what others expect you to do for them, you soon will exhaust yourself trying. Your priorities will become tomorrow's to do list. You will never have enough time today and you will put your dream and goals off for another tomorrow.

Suppose your child comes in at the last minute needing school supplies to do a project that is due tomorrow. You stop what you are doing and run to the nearest store to pick up the necessary items so your child won't receive a failing grade. Or how about those dear friends who repeatedly stop by unannounced and are always in the midst of a crisis?

What if your client waits until the last minute to contact you for work he needs completed immediately? In business, technology has greatly increased our ability to meet the demands and needs of others, theoretically in less time. It has also created an instant accessibility factor. Fax machines, cell phones and e-mail were all designed to make our lives easier. We depend on evolving technological advances and these products play an important role in our lives. However, they should serve us. If we allow ourselves to become caught up in each demand that is placed on us whenever the phone rings or the mailbox indicates new mail, then we are the servants.

As dependent as our business and personal lives have become on these wonderful devices, the perception of having instant access can place us in a position where people's expectations of us do not align with our priorities. People seek instant gratification and want an immediate response. The fax or e-mail sent five minutes ago may be followed by a phone call asking if it has been reviewed. People often forget that others are ahead of them. We then succumb to their needs in order to maintain our business and personal relationships. Many times we do so, however, at the expense of our own priorities and personal plan.

These distractions and interruptions are called life. Life happens. Things come up that aren't in the schedule. The key is to reduce the number and intensity of daily disruptions.

So how do you minimize the second LIE and maintain focus and priorities? First, protect your dreams and goals by creating boundaries. Know your own limits as to how much you can take on without sacrificing your priorities. Be clear with yourself so that you can be clear with others.

Second, communicate with those around you. Whatever role you play at the moment- parent, professional, employee, manager, significant other or spouse- it is imperative to let others know your priorities. By staying focused and communicating your needs, you will more easily prioritize the demands and needs of others. You may need time in the morning to pray, write or work. Or, you may require advance notice when projects are due or people are coming over to the house. Communicate with the people in your life to diminish the constant barrage of unexpected demands they may place on you. By communicating your priorities to your spouse, employees, clients or children, you are not saying that they are less important. You are allowing yourself the power to be more effective in your role.

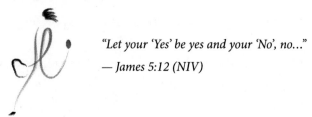

"Let your 'Yes' be yes and your 'No', no..."
— *James 5:12 (NIV)*

There is a simple communication technique for setting boundaries and maintaining priorities. Learn to say NO! This is a great life-management technique and it will prevent your participation in the second LIE. How many times have you spread yourself too thin with extra activities, meetings or projects? Recall and reclaim your power. As you empower yourself, you will place your priorities in proper order. Learn to say no to those people and those activities that aren't in your best interest. It is ironic that one of the first words that we learn to speak as a child is the word no and as adults we find it difficult to do so when it is in our best interest. Say no unless it is an absolute yes.

"Success depends on getting good at saying no without feeling guilty. You cannot get ahead with your own goals if you are always saying yes to someone else's projects."
— *Jack Canfield*

If you struggle with saying no, then allow a period of time between a request and your response in order to evaluate your answer. I have become involved in many things that were not in my best interest by saying the simple words, "Sure. Not a problem." I was then forced to deal with my aggravation. If I had taken time to reevaluate my priorities and the person making the request, "no" would have been easy. "I will have to get back to you," gives you the opportunity to assess the value of the request. If you fail to respect your priorities, you will not respect your dreams and goals. And, if you fail to respect your dreams and goals, those around you may do the same. Ultimately, you will not be on purpose.

LIE #3 – Instant Gratification

"Set your mind on things above, not earthly things."
— *Colossians 3:2 (NIV)*

The third LIE represents events, people or things which give you immediate satisfaction and instant gratification. This LIE is the pleasure principle. It can sneak up on you as quickly as the first and second LIEs to rob you of your Time and Focus. The participation in this LIE is more invasive, however, because it incorporates doing something that, in some way, makes you feel good. Do not mistake the third LIE with pleasurable activities that are consciously chosen, or times you may take during your day to recharge in some way. The third LIE involves intentionally creating a diversion to avoid dealing with a challenge or completing the task at hand.

Often times, we want to participate in the third LIE. We look for something to help us feel good, now. Making a phone call to catch up on the latest gossip or playing a game of solitaire on the computer at work feeds our need to be doing. At home, we may sit down to watch one program on television and find ourselves two hours later still flipping channels. Productive activities, such as cleaning the house or purging the files on your desk, have their proper place. However, when you use them as a prerequisite for initiating your more significant actions, then you avoid doing your top priority. This avoidance is a form of self-sabotage and, although you may believe you are involved in constructive behavior, you again are involving yourself in a LIE.

The Dynamic "Ds"

"Dost thou love life? Then do not squander time, for that is the stuff life is made of."
— *Benjamin Franklin*

Every action uses energy. Ironically, every action you deliberate over also depletes your mental and physical energy. When faced with a challenging situation or mastering your goals, make calculated decisions regarding what is necessary. Then, prioritize your list before initiating any action. Maintaining your priorities and taking purposeful and productive actions towards mastering your goals and manifesting your dreams conserves your Time, Focus and, ultimately, your energy.

THE DYNAMIC "D"s

1) DELETE

2) DELEGATE

3) DEFLATE

4) DEFER

5) DO

I developed a series of questions to determine whether or not my actions are purposeful and productive. They assist me through challenges when I need to define what is of paramount importance for my Time and Focus. I also use them to keep me on course for achieving my goals and dreams. I call them my Dynamic Ds: Delete, Delegate, Deflate, Defer, and Do. Staging these concepts in the following questions will assist you in prioritizing your activities and give them the proper amount of Time, Focus and attention to direct your energy to the appropriate tasks.

Dynamic D #1: Delete

> "Things which matter most must never be at the mercy of things that matter least."
> — Johann Wolfgang von Goethe

The first D is Delete. "Does this really need to be done?" If, after thought and consideration, you realize that this action is not beneficial to a goal or dream, will not move you through an adversity or is necessary to manage a challenge, then the answer is no. The action is not worthy of your Time and Focus and you move on. If the answer is yes then you proceed to the next four stages of the Ds.

Dynamic D #2: Delegate

> "To achieve great things, two things are needed; a plan, and not quite enough time."
> —Leonard Bernstein

The second D is Delegate. "Do YOU really need to do this or is there someone else that could take care of the matter?" Every good manager and executive knows the necessity of delegating. This does not mean you expect someone else to do your work or handle your responsibilities. This question, however, will prevent you from engaging in activities or volunteering for the purpose of avoidance, people-pleasing and all other techniques we use to get off-course. This question will also allow you to relinquish control.

Adversity is difficult enough. However, it becomes easy to sabotage ourselves when we are in the process of making our dreams our reality as well. We pile so much into a day and take on added responsibilities, duties and workload. If we are into people-pleasing, we may attempt to make ourselves indispensable by taking on too much and relieving others of their responsibilities. We try to fit 48-hours into a 24-hour day and we always come up short. We are out to prove that we can do it all personally and professionally.

Delegating in your personal life can be as easy as having someone clean your house while you pursue a new endeavor or class. I relinquished the responsibility of mowing the lawn. In actuality, someone else took the responsibility away from me when the mower was stolen from my property. I didn't mind mowing. The lawn was actually pasture land and the hours required to mow gave me time to zone out to the hum of the engine. When the mower was stolen, however, I hired a service to do the job. This allowed me time to do things I wanted to do on the weekends. I spent time riding my horse and relaxing on a trail ride. In the heat of summer, while someone else cut my grass, I took a yoga class. I filled that time with activities that were beneficial to my physical and mental well being.

Delegating in your professional life insures that you release to others their responsibilities and duties. I worked with a client who was overwhelmed in her professional capacity and on the verge of burn out. She had ulcers, headaches and her taxed immune system allowed her to catch whatever germ floated around in the office. Many times, she worked 20 hours in a day and slept on the sofa in her office. In the morning, she changed into clothes she kept in her car.

If it is your goal to excel in the corporate world, understand that there may be temporary sacrifices in other areas of your life. The key word here, however, is temporary. Creating this type of working environment for the long haul is a schedule, not a life. In the case of my client, I reviewed her work habits. She had assistants and other professionals working with and for her. However, she was so conscientious and controlling, she failed to properly utilize their talents and delegate to them their proper responsibilities. My job was to encourage her to let go and allow them to do their respective jobs. She began to delegate and review their work, and found she was more productive in less time. Having the opportunity to regain a healthy sleeping pattern and to reclaim her weekends, she regained and reclaimed her life.

Lack of delegation and the desire to be in control contributed greatly to the deterioration of my marriage. I have shared with you that I was affected by Hurricane Charley days after returning with my husband from our honeymoon. Dealing with the effects of the storm and the loss of my house gave a new meaning to the phrase, "The honeymoon's over."

My former husband was a contractor and contractors were in great demand during that chaotic time. However, rather than have his workmen and subcontractors repair the house in a timely manner, he decided we would do most of the work ourselves.

We spent every weekend working on the house. Friday and Saturday nights were spent in home improvement stores to pick up supplies for the next day. Eight months into the process and no end in sight, I suggested we make a plan and bring in reinforcements to complete the repairs. He refused.

My former husband had great vision but no ability to formulate a strategy. Much of the work was beyond his physical capabilities and talents to complete correctly. It was definitely beyond mine! After living in a motor home for 14 months, I fired him from the job. Relieving him from his position instantly promoted me from wife/worker to ex-wife/supervisor. Trust me, I delegated!

Dynamic D #3: Deflate

"The future is something that everyone reaches at the rate of sixty minutes an hour, whatever he does, whoever he is."
— C. S. Lewis

The third D of the Dynamic Ds is Deflate. "Does this really have to be done this way?" In other words, are you giving this activity too much intensity and exaggerating its importance? In our enthusiasm or desire to feel significant, we may tend to create a mountain when a molehill would have sufficed.

I enjoy entertaining company and acting as the consummate hostess. By no means a gourmet cook, I take pleasure in creating an extensive and fun menu. People who come to my home never fill their own glasses and never remove their plates from the table. They are guests. My kitchen is clean before the last food item is finished cooking. Through all of my preparation and detail, I am usually worn out by the end of the evening.

One Thanksgiving I decided to cook and invite all my friends who had no place to spend the holiday. This was an idea that sounded good the moment that it popped into my head, but by the time it was implemented, I questioned my sanity. I expected 19 guests. In my family, Thanksgiving always meant too much food on the table. Between my mother, my grandmother and me, we had a number of cooks in the kitchen and always prepared a variety of different dishes.

I wanted to recreate that table setting of food for my friends. Instead of one type of potato, there were four. Rather than one green vegetable, there were three. There were also four pies, a cake and a banana pudding. Thankfully, I set dinner for 5:00 p.m. I had overextended myself and called my mother to help me finish cooking.

At the end of the evening, dinner was great and everybody had a good time. However, I was so tired I couldn't wait for the last guest to leave so I could get into a hot shower and then bed. In retrospect, everyone, including myself, would have enjoyed dinner just as much had I chosen to deflate it. A smaller menu on the table would have been just as enticing and would have allowed me a greater opportunity to celebrate the holiday with my friends and family.

Even time off can be deflated. Vacations become work when you feel the need to take every excursion off the ship or every tour that leaves from the hotel. You squeeze in shopping at the local boutiques or tourist traps before you rush off to make your reservation at the in restaurant. I have had the opportunity to travel to beautiful places and experience fabulous sites. I have been on the tours and dashed to get to dinner before they gave away the reservation. Once home, I have felt in need of another vacation.

The word vacation comes from its Latin roots meaning freedom. I have reached that point in my life where I do not feel the need to squeeze everything into one break. I have made the conscious decision to deflate my vacations and allow them to serve me for the purpose for which they are intended. They are a break from daily life and a chance to rest and experience the gifts of a different location.

There are several places that I return to during my time off to recharge and refresh my energy. One of my favorites is Sedona, Arizona. I enjoy spending time in the red rock mountains. While I am there, I have no set schedule. I wake up and enjoy my morning meditation. Then I get dressed and walk to the coffee shop. Sipping my coffee, I take in the sights and sounds. From there, I visit the museum, or embark on a hike or take a class given by a local instructor. I may take a tour or two, or hire a personal guide to explore things I haven't seen. I love shopping, walking the sidewalks and talking with the merchants. In the time I am there I am at rest.

Projects in your professional life can also be daunting and in need of deflating. We may take on an assignment with great enthusiasm. In our anticipation, we may make extensive plans for the project's implementation and completion. And then, we may jump into it with gusto. The challenge is that the task at hand may not deserve or need the intensity with which we channel our energy towards its achievement. Our eagerness may leave other more significant goals lacking our Time and Focus, and energy.

Deflating a professional assignment or a task towards accomplishing a goal or dream does not mean failing to do your absolute best. It means that you assess what needs to be done. Your assessment will determine each action as either necessary or superfluous. If it is redundant or serves no worthwhile purpose to the project, then you reduce the size of the task and turn your energies towards those things which will serve your goals and dreams.

Deflating the daunting tasks at hand will also keep you from feeling overwhelmed and allow you to manage your Time, Focus and energy when you are in the middle of a major challenge, transition or adversity. At the time that I fired my husband and took over the repair of my house, I faced an unlivable structure still in shambles. The only way I could handle this challenge was to deflate it by breaking it into smaller projects. Each project was prioritized and managed individually, rather than focusing on the whole house. In this manner, piece by piece, the repair was completed.

Dynamic D #4: Defer

"It is not for us to forecast the future, but to shape it."
— *Antoine de Saint-Exupery*

The fourth of the Dynamic Ds is Defer. "Does this really need to be done NOW?" Is this action or task the thing that you should do at this precise moment, or is it more appropriate to defer it to another time? This is not the same as procrastination. We sometimes get ahead of ourselves in our plans or make too many plans at one time. This causes confusion and feelings of failure when you do not have the hours in the day or the knowledge at hand to juggle all that you are attempting to do. This question, like the others, keeps you honest about your priorities and where you are on your path.

Dynamic D #5: Do

"Do everything without complaining or arguing."
— *Philippians 2:14 (NIV)*

The last of the Dynamic Ds is Do it. If you can't Delete, Delegate, Deflate or Defer, then it is appropriate that you proceed, without hesitation or procrastination, to Do it. Each moment is an investment in your life.

The manner in which you choose to spend it will determine the return on your investment.

The Dynamic Ds are a tool to insure that the *PowerShift* of Time and Focus is utilized towards the furthering of the mastering of your goals, the manifesting of your dreams and to live your life in purpose. You only have 24 hours in each day. The Dynamic Ds make them count and encourage you to be accountable to make living a life of significance your priority.

To live in purpose and fulfill the destiny of your dreams and goals, you must engage Time and Focus as the powerful forces they are. Time and Focus shape your life and create a *PowerShift*!

"The whole life of man is but a point of time; let us enjoy it."
— *Plutarch*

PowerShift Reflections - The dominant theme of your today will write the story you live tomorrow. Despite whatever challenges or setbacks invade your life, you have the Time and Focus to direct your energy and awareness.

CHAPTER
SEVEN

POWERSHIFT: WORDS & THOUGHTS

"My thoughts are nothing like your thoughts," says the Lord.
"And my ways are far beyond anything you could imag-
ine. For just as the heavens are higher than the earth, so my
ways are higher than your ways and my thoughts higher than
your thoughts."
— Isaiah 55:8-9 (NLT)

Our minds serve as the custodians of our spiritual energy. The Words and Thoughts that are processed in our minds become the caretakers of our souls. They are the guardians of our greatness and should reflect the significance of our spirit. Both our greatest limitations and achievements are experienced through the power of the Words that are spoken to, and by us, as well as through the Thoughts we mentally manage. Success and failure, significance and defeat begin in the mind. When they are used to overcome challenges, master your goals, manifest your dreams and live in purpose, Words and Thoughts are a *PowerShift*!

In order to live a life in purpose and create the *PowerShift*, you must respect the authority Words and Thoughts have in your mind. Words and Thoughts can create new ideas and concepts to support your goals and dreams. They can also become your greatest handicap. When you go through uncomfortable transitions in your life or face challenges, it becomes easy to speak Words and think Thoughts of defeat and hardship. The Words and Thoughts you entertain are measured against your internal value system.

From there, they are composed into opinions, judgments, beliefs and emotions. You must choose only those Words and Thoughts that will support your efforts to overcome the adversity, move you through the transition, master your goals and manifest your dreams.

Words and Thoughts have the intrinsic ability to determine the course of your life. Psychologists estimate that we may have as many as 60,000 thoughts each day. Of those, approximately 95% are repeated daily and 80% are negative. If these studies are accurate, that leaves us with a small minority of our thoughts working to encourage and support us.

By repeating the same negative thoughts daily, you are destined to create the same reality you are experiencing at this very moment. If you are not living the life you envision today, you have the ability to change your experience tomorrow. Your past does not have to dictate your future. In order to *Shift the Power* and live a life in purpose, your Words and Thoughts today must reflect the reality that you intend to create. Reality will eventually catch up.

Words and Thoughts have the power to affect and stimulate energy, impacting far beyond the present. Their tremendous influence is evident in phrases and statements that deliver their energy long past their first use. If you doubt the power of Words and Thoughts, recall some of the most famous statements and the changes they produced. "I have a dream" were words delivered by Martin Luther King, Jr. in 1963, embracing the thought that blacks and whites could live together equally and peacefully. This phrase was spoken in an era of civil discord and gave energy and sustenance to the civil rights movement. These power-filled words continue to inspire and educate to this day.

"As a person thinks in his heart so is he."
— *Proverbs 23:7*

Take a moment and think about the power of mind. Like a computer, the mind processes thousands of inputs per day. It intercepts and interprets facts and feelings and can multi-task to run formulas and figures. Just imagine what you could accomplish if the majority of what you entered was pertinent, purposeful and positive! The power of the mind is only as effective as the stimuli it engages. Garbage In Garbage Out is as relevant to the Thoughts you think and the Words you speak as it is to the data you enter into your desktop computer.

The operating system of the mind works on both a conscious and unconscious level. Each level has its own distinct purpose and functions. The conscious level represents our awareness. It is the ability of the mind to process, analyze and memorize, and allows us to acknowledge our experiences while we experience them. The conscious mind can be influenced by our values and beliefs, race, culture and environment.

The unconscious level is our storage center, saving data we collect. Through the information it has amassed during the course of our lives, the unconscious mind gives us the ability to inadvertently respond and react to stimuli. Often times, we do so without true awareness. This system of the mind allows us to recall how something made us feel. We may remember the mood, the emotion or the atmosphere, although we may not be able to remember the exact circumstance surrounding the memory.

You have a unique ability to control the conscious and unconscious mind. Properly programmed with positive, constructive thoughts of your goals and dreams, this operating system can assist you in drawing to you what you desire. How do you take authority over your conscious and unconscious mind? Begin at the end. Knowing the results you want to produce transforms the energy of your spoken Words and the power of your Thoughts. Reprogram your mind and begin to make your dreams a reality.

"It is the same with my word.
I send it out, and it always produces fruit.
It will accomplish all I want it to,
and it will prosper everywhere I send it."
— Isaiah 55:11 (NLT)

There is a magnetic energy in the mind that can attract our most dominant thoughts to us. This universal force has the ability to draw to you that which you constantly think about, or on which you contemplate or meditate. Therefore, you must think and speak in terms of the goals you want to master and the dreams you desire to manifest. And, you must do so despite your present circumstances.

If you want to create health and prosperity in your life, you must think in terms of abundance. Focusing on the lack of money in your wallet or where you fall short in your bank statement will not improve your situation. You will continue to experience the same or similar conditions and situations in your life if your Words and Thoughts are directed to the deficiencies in your bank account.

If you want to manifest love into your life, shift your thoughts to the person that you want to attract. Be specific as to his or her qualities and attributes. Focusing your Words and Thoughts on the pain of past relationships and lamenting over your hurt and grief can attract similar types of people and associations into your life.

If you want to promote yourself professionally, think in terms of your gifts, talents and abilities. Review what you have already accomplished and project what you desire to achieve. Focusing on your lack of formal training or education or another person's abilities will keep you at the same professional level.

Does this mean that one negative thought or a bad day or week will contradict all your power thinking? Not anymore than one cookie will destroy an entire diet. If you continue, afterwards, to watch what you eat and maintain a healthy lifestyle, then your eating program remains intact and on course. The damage begins when you continue to eat one cookie after another.

It is the same with your thoughts. One or two negative thoughts will not counteract all your affirmations and positive energy. There are times when you will be down. We live in a fast-paced society and a multitasking lifestyle. Sometimes, it is hard to keep up mentally and physically. When we are tired, it is easy to become discouraged and experience temporary thoughts of defeat.

Discouragement is not a mortal sin. It is human nature to experience the wide range of emotions God has given us. Allow yourself permission to be human and to just be. However, just as you have to make a conscious decision to put down the bag of cookies, you must consciously begin to flow positive energy into your Words and Thoughts.

"Our life always expresses the result of our dominant thoughts."
— *Soren Kierkegaard*

There are times when our goals and dreams seem out of reach. Negative emotions and random thoughts may rise to the surface and we feel unhappy and depressed. There are other times when we face adversity and challenges, and destructive Words and Thoughts fuel the fear, apprehension and other unhealthy emotions.

Words and Thoughts possessing negative energy become dangerous when they remain in your mind. The presence of this force can create a defeated attitude and weaken your ability to face adversity and negotiate challenges. Your passion towards your purpose may diminish and the enthusiasm to achieve your goals and manifest your dreams may dwindle. Your mental and spiritual energy source can become compromised, further extinguishing your power. Getting through the day will take great effort. Such continuous energy can lead to a state of depression and anxiety. The cycle is further perpetuated through an overall general sense of failure which can pervade your entire being. Left unchecked, your health, finances and relationships may be affected.

You must overcome the tendency to default to the negative and engage in self-sabotage. When you experience this drain of energy, a mental and verbal tune-up may be in order. Become aware of what you are saying and thinking. Once you acknowledge any destructive Words and negative Thoughts dispose, discard and dissolve those that aren't furthering you towards your purpose. Give thanks for what they have shown you about yourself and the circumstance, and then release them.

When I made the conscious choice to recover from anorexia, I had to be conscientious with my Words and Thoughts. Every bite of food I placed in my mouth could provoke a thinking pattern such as, "I am getting fat," or "I am losing control." These words may not sound serious out of context, but for a person fighting anorexia, conquering these thoughts is the difference between recovery and relapse. If I wanted to get well, I had to take authority over my Words and Thoughts and not permit such statements to enter my mind or leave my lips. My previous self-programming had to be rejected and replaced with Words and Thoughts that sustained my conviction to return to a state of health and well-being.

Some people choose to put themselves down and utilize self-deprecating words as a result of low self-worth. Others do so in an effort to gain attention. They believe that in belittling and criticizing themselves, someone will speak up in their defense. The only person who can defend you from negative Words and Thoughts is you. Constantly telling yourself that you will never succeed, are not smart enough or don't have enough education may cause you to act in accordance with those Words and Thoughts. If you put yourself down and think poorly of yourself, you will attract other people who see you in the same manner and judge your abilities at the level of the self-image you create. If you think about problems, you will continue to manifest problems. If you think on negative things, you will attract negative things into your life. Thinking that you will never get through a challenge or you don't measure up against whatever adversity you are facing, will only make the getting through that much more difficult.

The days and weeks after Hurricane Andrew were stressful and challenging. My home and belongings were destroyed and my mother and I slept in my truck. The mosquitoes and the heat were unbearable. Day-to-day survival became the immediate goal. There was much publicity and criticism that the local, state and federal governments failed to act promptly in the disaster-torn area. For the most part, there was little direction or guidance for the first few weeks after the disaster.

During this critical time, I did not have the mental luxury to say, "I can't get through this," or "I don't have the ability to deal with this." Yes, there was stress, discouragement and fear. However, when faced with life-threatening circumstances, survival instincts can override insecurities. You can say, "I'll get through this," and "I have the strength and ability to handle this." If the power of your Words and Thoughts can strengthen and sustain you in the worst of challenges, think of their power in mastering your goals and manifesting your dreams!

Bad things do happen and it is impossible and unrealistic to ignore the challenges, adversity, devastating events or the fact that you're having a bad day. I have heard people say, "If I can get through this, then I will be happy." The reality of the matter is that you will not get through this until you change your Words and Thoughts and be happy. When a negative thought enters your mind, disrupt the flow of the energy before it settles in. Thinking and speaking negatively about yourself or your abilities sends the energy of those Words and Thoughts to interact with the world, possibly returning with more negative results. Thinking and speaking positively, on the other hand, allows those Words and Thoughts to interact with the universal energy, returning with positive results. Become aware of your Words and Thoughts and use them to create your life rather than to create further stress and anxiety in your life.

"Guard your heart above all else, for it determines the course of your life."
— Proverbs 4:23

We have determined that allowing negative Words and Thoughts to saturate our minds will only create further negative emotions. These emotions, continuing to react and respond to the further flow of negative stimulus, can lead to severe physical or mental health issues and additional negative situations. It is a simple process. Negative Thoughts can lead to negative Words. Negative thinking and speech patterns can distort the decision-making process. Poor decisions bring on poor outcomes, resulting in further negative Words and Thoughts. The cycle continues and situational insanity becomes a way of interacting in life. If we want to Shift our Power to experience the realization of our greatness, we must set up strategies to interrupt the process and establish solid habits of positive thinking and affirmative speech.

Once in place, constantly practicing the strategies and techniques will enhance your ability to counteract negative Words and Thoughts and build up your internal defense system. Whatever happens around you, you will be able to choose the right Words and Thoughts about the event, person or moment. You will realize that you cannot always physically change the outcome of a situation, but you can always change the manner in which you speak and think about it.

Over time, you will find you are no longer susceptible to the destructive influences of negative Words and Thoughts. You will able to guard your heart and mind and, in doing so, guard your goals and dreams as well. Focusing on God and speaking positive Words over the gifts and blessings in your life will enhance your ability to manifest more positive energy in your soul and spirit. As you cultivate positive Words and Thoughts you will reap the benefits of the *PowerShift*.

"Set your minds on things above,
not on earthly things."
— *Colossians 3:2 (NIV)*

How do you overcome the destructive and negative and replace it with the constructive and positive? It sounds too simple to say "just choose." Choose to think about what you do have, rather than what you do not have. Think about your unique gifts, talents and abilities, rather than about what you can't do. Focus on the solution and the options and opportunities, rather than the problem, challenges and obstacles. Contemplate what is possible, rather than what is impossible. Set your mind on God's greatness. In doing so, you will realize your own.

When negative Thoughts enter your mind or negative Words leave your lips, interrupt the energy with an affirmation or scripture. This topic has been addressed in a previous chapter, but it is a technique that bears repeating. Affirmations are positive statements. Said repeatedly with passion and consistency, these words and statements will change the thought-producing processing system in your mind. In altering how your mind thinks, you alter your life. For example, if your mind produces thoughts such as, "I will never get this done. I just don't have the ability," affirm words such as, "I have all the ability that I need and I am well able to accomplish this task." Although it may take time, you will find that your confidence in yourself and your abilities will increase.

Using scripture is also a great way to affirm the positive. For example, if you feel overwhelmed and experience thoughts of inadequacy, turn your thoughts towards your blessings, talents and gifts by affirming, "I can do all things through Christ who strengthens me," (Philippians 4:13). If you find yourself tired and thoughts are penetrating your mind trying to convince you that you just don't have what it takes, affirm, "They that wait upon the Lord shall renew their strength; they shall mount up with wings as eagles; they shall run, and not be weary; and they shall walk, and not faint," (Isaiah 40:31). If you can't recall a scripture or think of an affirmation, keep it simple and calm the stormy sea of thoughts in your mind and say, "Peace be still," (Mark 4:39).

Another technique to shift your thoughts is to choose a Power-Word for the day. This is a Word that signifies whatever quality you need to complete a project, affirm faith in yourself, instill a trait or characteristic or bring your mind back on track. PowerWords are words such as "courage," "passion," "peace," "joy," "focus," and "forgive." If you find yourself thinking negative thoughts or using words of defeat, immediately interrupt their flow by repeating your PowerWord.

There is another technique effective for stopping negative thoughts when they enter your mind. At the moment you acknowledge mentally processing a negative or destructive thought, use the words "cancel, cancel," "scratch that," or "delete." I have a computer program I use for dictation. I speak into a microphone and my words appear on my computer screen. If I am in mid-sentence and want to change my thought, I tell it, "scratch that," and the words disappear from the page. Your mind is like the computer and will process whatever your thoughts dictate. Scratch negative Thoughts, delete negative Words and cancel negative processes from your mind.

> "A man is but the product of his thoughts. What he thinks, he becomes."
> — Mahatma Gandhi

You must also cancel and delete any negative Words and Thoughts spoken over you by others. It is easy to allow another's destructive statement to enter your mental processing system. Once it permeates your mind and becomes a part of the analysis process, it can diminish your self-esteem or cause you to doubt your abilities. In order to limit your exposure to the influence of this negative energy, you must disassociate yourself from the Words and Thoughts.

I have had negative Words and Thoughts spoke over me by my brothers. My brothers are my thought thieves. In our conversations, they attempt to rob me of my positive thoughts and replace them with thoughts to sabotage my self-esteem. Their comments and statements are negative and toxic in nature. Once I have left their presence, I detoxify my thought patterns.

One day, during a discussion regarding the care of my father, one of my brothers demanded to see my bank statements. My disabled father lived with, and was under the financial and physical care of my mother and me. I am a self-sustaining, professional woman. My brother had not contributed financially to the health care, maintenance or support of my father. I advised him that my finances were not his business unless he wanted to share his finances with me, as well. Frustrated that I would not comply with his demand, my brother replied, "It is my business because when you run out of money, I will have to step in."

When I run out of money? How dare anyone speak such destructive Words and place such negative Thoughts in my mind and energy. As a single, professional woman, I chose to participate in the care of my elderly, disabled father. Neither of my brothers, despite the availability of their resources, chose to do so.

This statement was irresponsible, toxic and potentially detrimental to my confidence. My first response was anger and total contempt for his failure to be a supportive sibling. My thoughts of anger immediately turned to fear as my mind seized the statement and began analyzing the possibilities. Suppose I do run out of money? What if something happens to me and I can't provide for my parents? What if I prove my brother right? How will I take care of my responsibilities? The words, "When you run out of money," haunted me.

I knew this downward spiral had to stop immediately. The negative thought process undermined my self-worth and the doubts could eventually undermine my abilities to manifest financial abundance. I did not want to allow his words to become a self-fulfilling prophecy. I reminded myself that I have a divine bank account that has never run dry. God has always protected, provided for and given me the abilities and opportunities to provide for those I love and who depend on me. When I heard my brother's words in my head, I said to myself, "STOP! CANCEL! DELETE!" I replaced his irrational statements with affirmations of positive abundance. "I am the rich child of a loving Creator." I reminded myself of the scripture, "I have come that they may have life, and have it to the full," (John 10:10 NIV). It doesn't say, "I have come that they may have life until they run out of money."

It is not uncommon for those closest to us to speak negative Words and Thoughts over us. Some teenagers I have coached said that they have been told by parents, siblings or others of influence in their lives, "You are such a screw-up," or "You'll never amount to anything." Many adults can recall similar childhood memories. These Words and Thoughts can have a detrimental impact on a person's future. If you have ever experienced this type of negative thought pattern introduced by a family member, friend or teacher, first and foremost remember that you are a child of God. You are blessed with the unique and Divine gifts of the Father. Affirm His Greatness in your life. Affirm your own Greatness as His creation. Release those negative Words and Thoughts and replace them with Words and Thoughts of the life that God intends for you to live.

"The tongue can bring death or life;
those who love to talk will reap the consequences."
— *Proverbs 18:21 (NLT)*

Guarding your mind is also making a conscious choice to avoid group gossip. We can share physical germs from mouth to mouth. We can also share negativity germs from mouth to mouth. Negative Words and Thoughts are like a bad cold. The germs are easily shared and can contaminate others. The symptoms of these infectious Words and Thoughts can make you feel miserable. Preventative medicine is the best.

One of my mother's friends came up with a short and simple way to end gossiping when it began in her group. If someone spoke negatively or gossiped about another person, she replied, "Well, that's neither here nor there," and walked away. No one knew the meaning of this simple statement, but it interrupted the flow of the discussion. She was able to leave the situation without contributing to or judging the conversation.

"Avoid all perverse talk; stay away from corrupt speech."
— *Proverbs 4: 24(NLT)*

Another source of negative Words and Thoughts can be found in that which we read or watch. The media, whether in written, visual or audible form, can have a profound effect on our Words and Thoughts. The substance of much of this material is developed to entice the senses and sell to the masses and has no benefit to a positive speech or thought pattern.

It is not necessary to turn off the television and stereo. It is, however, important to be conscious of what is called entertainment and the seeds that are planted in your mind. If you are not conscious of the content that is broadcast to your mind, images can be created and thoughts can be formed without any discerning process on your part. In short, if you are not thinking for yourself, it will be done for you.

Many television programs and movies hypnotize you with violent storylines filled with vivid, gruesome images. Their visually dramatic accounts can conjure up images in your mind and evoke emotions that will affect your thoughts. Your mind cannot differentiate from what is real and imagined. Those images can be replayed time and again in your mind's eye and the thoughts developed from those scenes can drain your energy.

There were several dramatic television programs I enjoyed watching as background entertainment while in the middle of doing other things. I followed the story lines off and on for several seasons without giving much attention to the exact content.

I made a decision to turn these programs off and change the energy in the house. If I wanted background noise, I turned on a sitcom, sports or music. Months later, I sat down to unwind and flipped the channels to the programs I had once watched. They were filled with graphic scenes depicting vicious murders, women and children being raped, and other heinous crimes. The pictures were up-close and personal. I felt the energy in my body change from peace and well-being to tension and fear. I was no longer numb to their effects of the story lines or immune to the violent segments.

Do these types of graphic storylines occur each day in reality? Unfortunately, they do. However, I made a conscious choice not to permit this negative content to be broadcast in my mind and affect my thoughts.

Dramatic series and movies are not the only product on television that can affect your thought process. There are a multitude of talk shows, reality shows, news programs and documentaries that fill primetime TV. Navigating through these shows requires being a participating spectator in order to distinguish fact from fantasy and truth from propaganda. Failure to do so may result in accepting the opinions and stories of those who designed the topic for a specific spin or to hype a particular person or product. You may find yourself repeating opinions and viewpoints, or accepting information without testing the veracity of the statements made.

The same guidelines should be adhered to when reading various publications. Many of the articles that you read in newspapers and magazines can alter your thought pattern. Sex, celebrity and sensationalism sells. It sells because we read it. Do not allow another person's position on a subject to become yours without considering the source and whether or not it is in alignment with your beliefs and values. I ask that you read this book in the same manner. You may not fully adopt the concepts or my views may not fully resonate with yours. That's okay because it means that you are actively reading and not allowing someone to place concepts in your mind without processing them against your belief system.

Music also affects your thoughts and emotions because it can make you feel strong and upbeat or bring you to tears. The lyrics can encourage you to feel anger or they can make you smile. Songs can take you back to a place and time when life was happy or they can remind you of sadness and despair. Music can be affirmations to a melody. Be aware of the lyrics to which you listen and the words you repeat over when you sing.

Again, I am not suggesting that you turn off the television and stereo or throw away your CDs and cancel your magazine subscriptions. What I am saying, however, is that your mind, like your body, needs to be supplemented with good nutrients in order to produce positive thoughts. You cannot live on junk food and expect your body to perform at optimum levels. In the same manner, you cannot fill your mind with tabloid TV and lurid lyrics and expect your thoughts to perform to your level of greatness.

The airwaves do contain upbeat music and provocative talk shows. There are series that are entertaining and documentaries that are educational. There are fiction and nonfiction books, classic and contemporaries that fill the shelves and books on tape and CDs that can make drive time enjoyable, informative and productive. It is your conscious choice to choose that which will guard your mind, initiate positive thoughts and Shift your Power.

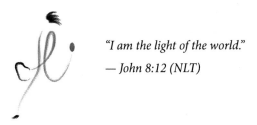

"I am the light of the world."
— *John 8:12 (NLT)*

There is no greater power in the spoken word to affect your being than the words "I am." The phrase defines and describes us in the instant we speak or think it. I am can serve as a constructive affirmation of your self-worth and empowerment or as a destructive assertion of the perceived shortcomings, flaws and failures of your character.

Speaking the words, "I am" into your being labels and categorizes you. The words that follow this definitive statement must be selected with care and caution. Affirmations such as, "I am well-qualified for this job," or "I am gifted in this area," are positive affirmations that define you and will promote a positive performance. Negative affirmations such as, "I am never going to get anywhere in my life," or "I am such a loser," will prevent you from attaining the best the universe has to offer. Do not set yourself up for a self-defeat by your choice of words.

All of us have made silly mistakes or done something without thinking and said, "I'm so stupid," and laughed it off. By itself, this will not cause your mental being any damage or distress. However, at the point where the negative words become associated with the negative emotions, they combine to create a destructive force. The negative emotions and words feed off each other's energy to sustain the damage until you make a conscious decision to interject positive thoughts and words to counteract the detrimental effects.

Often it is easier to create a negative label of ourselves than it is to create one that is positive. We find it more comfortable to be critical of ourselves than to find ourselves worthy of praise. It is easier to say, "I am so fat," or "I am getting old," than to celebrate ourselves for the gifted individuals we are. Once you identify yourself with the words, "I am," it becomes your reality.

During the time period when I had an eating disorder, I was diagnosed as being an anorexic. My disease now had a classification and my whole being became a part of, and perpetuated the definition, "I am an anorexic." I claimed it as my identity.

When the miracle of my healing from this disorder occurred, I had to release this identity in order to support my recovery. It was an identity born from a simple thought of, "I am fat," combined with a low self-esteem. Despite the detrimental effects of the disease on my physical body, my mind grabbed on to the I am of this illness as something unique and individual.

Liberating myself from this mental stronghold was not easy. The thought and statement of, "I am anorexic," had become embedded in my brain and nurtured for five years. It was who I was. Who would I be without this I am? Releasing this identity allowed me to let go of what I thought was my defining trademark. I realize that many addiction treatment programs require their participants to maintain the label of I am as part of the continued recovery process. It is not my intention to contradict their practices. It was my personal decision through a Divine intervention to release that part of my life and no longer identify myself with such a powerful and destructive description.

"I am the greatest, I said that even before I knew I was."
— *Muhammad Ali*

I had to create a new identity to maintain the gift of the miracle I experienced. I filled my mind with positive affirmations of I am. I am healthy, I am talented, I am a loving being, I am the blessed child of a loving Creator. I created the Thoughts and spoke the Words. In doing so, I defined and created my new reality.

Remember, you become the substance following the words "I am." Eliminate words such as depressed, tired, exhausted, and stressed from your daily vocabulary. How many times a day do you say, "I am stressed," or "I am tired"? If you say it enough, you will remain tired and stressed. Simply replace, "I am stressed," with "I am blessed," and experience an increase in your joy and productivity. Replace, "I am tired," with "I am wired," and see how much more energetic you can be!

"Let the weakling say, "I am strong!"
— *Joel 3:10 (NIV)*

Continue to take a powerful approach with I am and the words will serve you in a positive manner. Combine your high energy PowerWord with I am and repeat it throughout the day. I am passionate, I am courageous, I am enthusiastic. Use these positive affirmations to define your being and create your world. I am capable, I am an intelligent person, I am worthy. Use these words to *Shift the Power* in your life.

"Don't use foul or abusive language. Let everything you say be good and helpful, so that your words will be an encouragement to those who hear them."
— *Ephesians 4:29 (NLT)*

Motivating other people to perform to the peak of their greatness entails speaking positive words of approval and acceptance. The Words and Thoughts we introduce to those in our personal and professional environment have the energy to transform lives. Our words have the ability to influence the goals and dreams of others. As a friend, employer, parent, spouse, coach or any person who holds a position of authority over another, we have an obligation to respect their greatness and be responsible for the words we choose to speak over them.

These words not only have the energy to affect the moment at hand, but may have an impact that is far-reaching over and above the present circumstance and their original intention. When I was in middle school, a teacher wrote on a progress report that I didn't work well with others. I had a straight "A" average and received positive remarks on my conduct. This negative statement stayed in my thoughts throughout my scholastic career and influenced my behavior in other educational projects. Whenever there were assignments that involved group participation, it triggered the thought of the progress report and I repeatedly told myself that I didn't work well with others.

The truth was that I got along well with other people and enjoyed group interaction. I "didn't work well with others" because I preferred to work on projects by myself. I wanted to be the one responsible for the quality of work that I completed. I also wanted to work on my own schedule. To this day, I work for myself and, for the most part, by myself. What this teacher failed to see in me was my independent, entrepreneurial spirit.

How many people do we inadvertently brand with useless statements? You cannot continually refer to your spouse as a couch potato and expect projects to be completed around the house. You cannot call a child stupid or lazy and expect him or her to excel academically. It is not possible to deliver negative, destructive words over a person and receive any long-term, productive response.

This is not to say that poor performance is acceptable or that mistakes are permitted to go uncorrected. A *course correction* can be made without making a *coarse correction*. You can encourage a spouse to be more helpful around the house without making him or her feel household-chore challenged. A child can be told that their scholastic performance or conduct is inappropriate without demeaning their being. You can correct flaws in the work product of an employee and indicate proper behavior and outcomes in such a manner as to enable professional development. Make your expectations clear and choose words that are applicable to the situation rather than personal to the recipient. Statements that assault a person's character only degrade and humiliate. They are toxic attempts to control behavior through a negative verbal process that may ultimately lead to further deterioration in performance and in the relationship itself.

Public criticism also causes decline in a person's performance and self-esteem. Openly reprimanding or criticizing faults and failures in front of others humiliates and segregates people. Words of correction should be spoken in a confidential manner with every attempt made to find something positive and praiseworthy.

Praise is one of the most valuable tools in empowerment and self-development. Words of praise indicate that behavior or performance is acceptable. Expressions of approval reinforce self-worth and make a person feel that they are appreciated. Praise values both the person and the performance and develops character.

Above all, always end a personal or professional encounter on a positive thought. Don't leave other people talking about problems or with negative statements. Before you end a conversation, talk about solutions, speak words of encouragement and interject positive energy into the situation.

"Change your thoughts and you change your world."
— *Norman Vincent Peale*

Words and Thoughts empower you to overcome challenges, face adversity, master your goals and manifest your dreams. Words and Thoughts create a *PowerShift*!

PowerShift Reflection - God spoke the world into existence with the words "Let there be…" You have the authority and ability to choose your Words and Thoughts and, to therefore, choose the life you want to live.

CHAPTER
EIGHT

POWERSHIFT: PARTNERS & PARASITES

"Tell me what company thou keepst, and I'll tell thee what thou art."
— *Miguel de Cervantes*

Each day you encounter people in the different facets of your life. You engage them on a personal basis and you connect with them in your work environment. Whatever the purpose of the interaction, there is always an exchange of energy. The people who surround you have the ability to exert tremendous influence in your life. They can affect you through your challenges and adversity, as well as influence your path to your purpose and the achievement of your goals and dreams.

The type of influence, however, is determined by the energy that they release and your ability to either accept or deflect it. We have a human need to be accepted and acknowledged by our spouse, children, friends, family, peer group and employer. In meeting this need, there are those who will support and encourage you and there are those who will sabotage you. *The PowerShift Principle* realizes that there are people who are positive and can become Partners in your process of self-empowerment. There are also those whose negativity will suck the energy from you. These people are Parasites. Learning to differentiate the energies and identify your Partners and the Parasites creates a *PowerShift*!

"Be careful the environment you choose for it will shape you; be careful the friends you choose for you will become like them."
— *W. Clement Stone*

The state of your own empowerment can be measured by the people in your immediate environment. Their physical habits, emotional health, spiritual beliefs, and their energy have the potential to influence and affect you. It is up to you to choose the life you intend to live. You must know your purpose, choose the goals you want to achieve and decide on the dreams to which you will aspire. The people that participate in your life's purpose must be in alignment with these choices and decisions.

Let's say, for example, that you have found the home of your dreams and it is your goal to own it within the year. You must assess your financial statement and determine the amount of the down payment. You know that in order to qualify for the mortgage you must pay off certain credit cards, refrain from incurring further debt and save additional monies for the down payment.

During this process, it is important that you align yourself with people who have similar financial dreams and goals for themselves and will support your efforts. If you choose to involve yourself and spend time with those who have no financial responsibilities and who choose to spend their money indiscriminately, it may tempt you to do the same. This behavior will only keep your goal of owning the house out of your financial reach.

Likewise, if it is your dream to run a marathon or lose twenty pounds, then you align yourself with those who have the appropriate physical lifestyle and dietary habits. Associating with those who don't exercise, who spend their weekends partying or eat hot fudge sundaes for breakfast, will only disrupt your efforts to master your goals and manifest your dreams. Remember that you are not passing judgment on those people that choose to spend their weekends at the latest hot spots or eat ice cream first thing in the morning. There is nothing right or wrong for those that enjoy such activities. It may be that such behavior will not jeopardize their goals and dreams. They are on their own journey.

"Surround yourself with only people who are going to lift you higher."
— Oprah Winfrey

Who are your PowerShift Partners? They are the people you trust in times of adversity and challenges, as well as with your dreams and goals. They are individuals and groups that you can take into your confidence and trust with your life because if you choose to share with them your purpose, goals and dreams, that is exactly what you are doing.

PowerShift Partners are your cheering section and your fan club. Partners see the best in you when you are not able to see it in yourself. They believe in you when your belief in yourself has diminished. Partners can serve as a barometer for the development of your self-empowerment. Their comments are beneficial without being critical. Their suggestions are valuable without devaluing your self-worth. PowerShift Partners are not jealous or envious of what you want to achieve or have already accomplished. They are not threatened by your success or significance but, instead, embrace and celebrate it. Their presence in your life creates harmony.

In a true PowerShift Pairing, the exchange of energy is mutually beneficial to both parties. You are your partner's fan club and cheering section, seeing their best when they have lost their vision for themselves. You support your Partner in the mastery of their goals and the manifestation of their dreams. Their accomplishments do not diminish you. Your thoughts, words and actions towards them are positive and purposeful as you celebrate their successes and significance.

There are different types of *PowerShift* Partners. Some come into your life for a specific reason and remain for a brief stay. Others become life-long relationships, such as mentors, teachers and students. *PowerShift* Partners can be individuals, an organization or a group.

"In friendship and in love, the two side by side raise hands together to find what one cannot reach alone."
— *Kahlil Gibran*

THE DEFINITION OF A

POWERSHIFT PARTNER IS

A POSITIVE ASSOCIATION

PROMOTING PROGRESS ON

YOUR PATH AND PURPOSE

WHILE PROTECTING YOUR

PERSONAL EMPOWERMENT.

I created a personal *PowerShift* partnership with three of my friends. We get together one evening a week at a local restaurant and engage in what has become jokingly known as egg therapy. Although it sounds more like a diet trend than a self-help tool, egg therapy is a time to share, support, suggest, laugh and listen. The wait staff and cook at the restaurant have come to expect us at our appointed day and time. Our same booth is always available and our coffee, tea and water are at the table by the time we sit down. For the most part, we order the same thing each week, and the cook has completed the prep work when we walk through the door.

Egg therapy is named after a client and friend of mine who died at the age 43 from a massive heart attack. Diane's spiritual and emotional heart was large. She was such a giving and caring person, it is ironic that her physical heart was the cause of her death.

Basically disabled and alone, Diane had no true support group. Despite her solitude, Diane was a strong person. She defended the weak, children and animals. I spoke at her memorial service and mentioned that she engaged in egg therapy. There were a few chuckles from the crowd because several of the people in the audience had, on occasion, participated with her in this therapy. If someone had abused a defenseless animal or person, Diane purchased several cartons of eggs and improperly disposed of them on the perpetrator's property. This practice became known as egg therapy.

I do not condone or encourage this type of property damage. However, I share this story because Diane was alone and had no one she trusted. She was not close to her family and had few close friends. Diane had no *PowerShift* Partners in her life.

Several years after her passing, I ate dinner with a friend at a restaurant that served breakfast all day. We ordered eggs. My friend and I discussed our busy lives. On the drive home, we realized how therapeutic it had been to share and support each other. Remembering Diane, who had no source of emotional support, I coined the phrase of egg therapy to define our evening.

There are now four in the egg therapy group, ranging in age from the mid-thirties to early fifties. We share what has happened the previous week or things that have happened in our past. It is a safe environment where we say what is on our minds without fear of being judged or criticized. What happens at egg therapy stays in egg therapy. The matters we discuss are confidential and there is a positive and supportive exchange of energy. We laugh, cry and vent. We talk about husbands and ex-husbands, teenage children, our own teenage years and our hopes and dreams.

Egg therapy is a *PowerShift* Partnership. It is a group where there is an even exchange of energy that is mutually beneficial to all involved. At times, we challenge one another during our conversations and in our exchanges of ideas and comments. Using an objective viewpoint, we might invite each other to think or act differently towards a person or circumstance. Our exchanges stimulate creativity, stretch the imagination and elevate personal energy.

If there is an uneven exchange of energy among members of your group, it may possibly drain your energy. This is not a *PowerShift* Partnership. Quite frankly, if you're the smartest person in your group, then you have outgrown your group. If you are the main go to person in your group, then there is an unequal exchange of energy and you have outgrown your group.

There are *PowerShift* Partnerships that exist for specific areas of your life, such as your professional and career endeavors. This partnership may include participation in networking groups, membership in business associations or connecting with an individual who is a member of your peer group. There may be *PowerShift* Partnerships that align with a specific personal goal or dream. These individuals or groups may include participation in clubs or organizations. Either way, the partnership is based on the same concept of promoting progress on your path and purpose while protecting your personal empowerment. The key is that this partnership does not extend past the perimeter of your career, job, profession or specific goal.

Working as a business consultant for one of my clients, I had the opportunity to develop a boot camp for a physical fitness facility. The program was designed to challenge those already actively exercising and physically fit. At the same time, this program encouraged those who were less active and had recently started a regular work-out routine. The participant to trainer ratio was 3:1 to insure that everyone who participated received proper guidance and supervision to avoid over-exertion and injury.

The camp ran for three weeks, beginning every weekday at 5:00 a.m. For two hours, the group ran throughout local neighborhoods using a variety of bus stops, playgrounds and parks as their workout equipment. They returned to the gym exhausted, but exhilarated. All fitness levels participated. Trainers who led the group challenged those in excellent physical condition. Other trainers remained with those less physically fit. Despite their level of conditioning, each person had a goal to accomplish by the end of the three weeks.

An interesting phenomenon began by day four of camp. The individual desire to accomplish became a source of respect and developed into a common goal for the group. A *PowerShift* Partnership developed. Those individuals that were better conditioned completed their run and turned back to run with and motivate those who were slower. The athletic participants completed their exercise sets and stepped in to spot and encourage those with less strength and ability. Stronger members of the group became the cheering squad for the older, slower and less physically in-shape members.

At the end of the session, the entire group progressed physically and exceeded the trainers' goals and expectations. The group also exceeded their own goals and expectations. Through this *PowerShift* Partnership, the common purpose of the members, and their ability to positively promote one another, elevated them as a whole.

"Keep away from those who try to belittle your ambitions. Small people always do that, but the really great make you believe that you too can become great."
— *Mark Twain*

Living a life in purpose and achieving your goals can be energized and expedited by the presence of a mentor. A mentor is someone who is where you want to be, either in your personal or professional life. That person has already accomplished something similar to what you want to accomplish or whose purpose is in alignment with yours and is ahead of you on the path. You can learn from a mentor because he or she will challenge you, as well as guide your steps. A mentor is someone you can emulate. Their presence motivates and stimulates your energies. A mentor is a *PowerShift* Partner.

I met my mentor during my first year in sales. She was my office manager and she greatly impacted my productivity and sales report. However, her presence, the essence of what she represented, had a greater influence on my life. Her authority was always tempered with compassion and her professionalism was marked with grace and class. She never demanded respect from her employees due to her position, rather she earned it. Her professional character and accomplishments served as a model for my professional life.

When I applied to law school, I asked her to write my recommendation. She gladly obliged and wrote it with her trademark blend of professionalism and sincerity. Although she died shortly thereafter, her lessons of strong character and integrity have survived and continued to influence me through the *PowerShift* Partnership.

Find mentors and establish a *PowerShift* Partnership to help you accomplish what you want to do or be. If you want to write, join a writer's group and emulate someone who is already published. If you want to speak, find someone who has a speaking career. If you want to develop a specific attribute, find someone who already has that trait or characteristic and learn from them. Surround yourself with those people who have taken the steps ahead of you. Be in their energy. Access their experience, knowledge and habits to transcend adversity, master goals and manifest dreams.

One word of caution, choose your mentors carefully. Objectively review their qualifications. Evaluate their successes. What are their successes? Are they presently actively involved with their success or do they elaborate and embellish on past glories? How do they speak to you? Do they critique you? Or do they criticize you? A good mentor will tell you what you are doing wrong and right, and will do so with positive reinforcement.

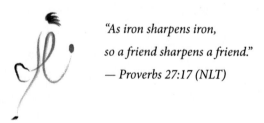

"As iron sharpens iron,
so a friend sharpens a friend."
— *Proverbs 27:17 (NLT)*

There are times when people are Divinely directed into our lives. Some enter our lives to teach us something that we need to learn. Others come to support us during a specific period. Sometimes the answers we are searching for come through people who step into our lives temporarily. They may have been through similar adversities or similar purposes. They come to create a *PowerShift* Partnership.

Not long after my divorce, I began dating again. I knew I was not ready to enter into another committed relationship. I knew I did not have the energy. The new man in my life had recently lost his spouse. We began dating and continued to do so for six months. We enjoyed each other's company; however, I had an intuitive feeling that this dating situation was only temporary.

I had been involved with a business partnership that turned sour. During the period of extricating myself from the legal and emotional turmoil, I appreciated his physical presence and emotional support. For the first time in my life, someone had my back. On the other hand, I taught him how to date again after having been in a long-term marriage. Together, we celebrated his birthday and the first holiday season after the passing of his spouse. I helped him through his difficult times and he helped me through mine. That was the purpose of the partnership. When it was complete, we left each other's lives.

"I will be your God throughout your lifetime—
until your hair is white with age. I made you, and I
will care for you. I will carry you along and save you."
— *Isaiah 46:4 (NLT)*

Above all, God is your primary *PowerShift* Partner. He is your Creator, He believes in you when you don't believe in yourself. He sees the greatness in you because He made you in His image. He has faith in you when you have lost faith in yourself and in Him. He is your cheering squad and fan club. He celebrates your successes and embraces your pain when you come up short. He knows what you want to accomplish because He put it in your heart. He is the ultimate support group and life coach.

"He who walks with the wise grows wise,
but a companion of fools suffers harm."
— *Proverbs 13:20 (NIV)*

On the opposite spectrum from the *PowerShift* Partners are the PowerSucking Parasites. These people are the skeptics and cynics. Do not dare to trust them with your purpose, dreams and goals. Their doubts and disbelief will drain your energy, poison your efforts and will suck the very vital life force from you.

If your *PowerShift* Partners are your cheering section, the PowerSucking Parasites are your jeering section. Their presence in your life is detrimental to your well-being personally and professionally. When you perform your best, they criticize. Your self- worth and self-empowerment threatens their security.

PowerSucking Parasites will protect their security at all costs to other people. Although they may camouflage themselves with syrupy, superfluous words, their comments are critical and may stick in your self-confidence. The detrimental diatribes of the Parasite attempt to diminish your self-worth and to elevate their self-esteem. PowerSucking Parasites are jealous and envious of your accomplishments and potential achievements. They are threatened by your success and intimidated by your significance. They may come in the form of a group or association, friends and clients. The Power-Sucking Parasite can even come under the guise of family members.

"They cannot take away our self-respect if we do not
give it to them."
— *Mahatma Gandhi*

PowerSucking Parasites want nothing more than to rob you of your self-esteem and self-respect. They will engage you only to sabotage your efforts. They can manipulate you into believing that what they are doing is for your promotion when their ulterior motive is to see you fail or to prevent them from failing. They are like a germ that invades your body when your immune system is weakened.

I was preparing to open my law practice in Miami on August 24th, 1992, the day that Hurricane Andrew hit South Dade. As I have already shared, I spent the next two years rebuilding my life. During this time, I met a woman who had owned her own law practice for a number of years. She offered me a job when I was financially struggling and living in a FEMA mobile home. She seemed like the answer to a prayer.

The answer to my prayer quickly turned into a demon in disguise. Although this attorney had been born into a wealthy family, she was jealous of me and made everything difficult. She was constantly angry in her personal life and displaced that anger at work by throwing temper tantrums. As her employee, I was required to take her dog to the vet and the groomers, to pick up the children from school and babysit. This wasn't in my job description as a lawyer.

On days she did not feel like working, she took me shopping to an upscale mall and spent thousands of dollars on designer clothes. Once, while on a shopping spree, she picked up a pair of designer slacks and sarcastically pointed out that they were my size and on sale. The pants cost more than what she paid me in a week.

She was a PowerSucking Parasite and I was in an abusive professional relationship. I thought I was in a position where I needed the job. The foundation of my security and self-confidence had already been shaken by the hurricane and the manner in which I had to live temporarily. Eleanor Roosevelt said, "No one can make you feel inferior without your consent." In this situation, I gave my consent. With that, I gave up all of my power.

My living arrangements in the FEMA mobile home were temporary. The damage she inflicted on me as a professional could have been permanent. I resigned from my job before I allowed myself to remain in a position where she would continue being a PowerSucking Parasite in my life. In her fury, she promised that I would never work in my city again. She was wrong. The lesson I had to remember was that this Parasite in my life only had the power I chose to give her.

"Love is patient, love is kind. It does not envy, it does not boast, it is not proud. It is not rude, it is not self-seeking, it is not easily angered, it keeps no record of wrongs. Love does not delight in evil but rejoices with the truth. It always protects, always trusts, always hopes, always perseveres."
— *1 Corinthians 13: 4-7 (NIV)*

When a member of the opposite sex professes love for you, it can be the sweetness of the most powerful elixir or it can be the poison of the most fatal toxin in your life. We speak of love in terms of commitment and in giving your heart to a special someone. That person can either be *PowerShift* Partner or a PowerSucking Parasite.

While in law school, I was involved with a man that I later realized was jealous of my educational pursuits and professional desires. Earlier in his own life, he had to withdraw from college because of his involvement with a parasitic group with which he associated.

His resentment of my education caused him to become a Power-Sucking Parasite. He always started an argument whenever I had a project due or was studying for exams in an effort to shift my attention away from my studies. I was under enough pressure in law school without having an outside force constantly attempting to sabotage my performance. Although I broke off the relationship several times, he always apologized and promised he would change. I believed him. Being a Parasite, he never did change. Prior to studying for the bar exam, I broke off the relationship with him permanently. He moved on to continue similar actions and behavior with his next girlfriend. She later became his wife, and then, his ex-wife.

It is not always easy to identify the PowerSucking Parasites in romantic relationships. There are going to be differences of opinions and different ways of doing things as two people attempt to join their lives together. There are good times and moments of sheer joy and there are bad times and agonizing pain. You must be able to identify the challenges that are a part of the union process and those confrontations that are disguised to seduce and seize your heart and soul.

A mutual friend introduced me to my former husband. Although, he came with good recommendations, he had been married several times. During our first lunch date, he told me that he was still married but separated from his wife. The divorce papers were prepared but never filed with the court. I had no desire to become involved with a man that was still attached to a spouse. This brief encounter was the end of our involvement. Or, so I thought.

Several months later, we were re-introduced. His divorce was being finalized and he asked me out to dinner. I accepted. From that point on, we had a whirlwind romance and I was engaged to be married. The wedding was set for later in the year, but he convinced me to move up the date and we were married a month later.

This man courted me. He said and did all of the right things. He showered me with attention. I received flowers every week. He liked my animals. He liked my parents. After remaining single for so many years, I thought that he was a gift from God.

He was a gift, but not the kind that I had envisioned. He was a lesson I needed to learn. Our marriage had little chance of surviving when Hurricane Charley struck our area six days after our return from our honeymoon. Such disasters are difficult enough on a marriage with a solid foundation, let alone when two people don't know each other. However, prior to the effects that the storm had on the marriage, the change in his personality became evident on the honeymoon. The hurricane only exacerbated the symptoms.

My husband was a controlling person. I soon saw the other side of him his previous wives had experienced. I fought for my emotional, spiritual and physical well-being as my husband attempted to dictate and control the repairs on my house, the clients I worked for and the friends I socialized with.

I had been an independent woman for the majority of my life. I experienced great stress and tension as I attempted to navigate though marital waters and his sea of chaos. He became emotionally and verbally abusive when he realized he could not control me. He walked out on me no less than six times within the first four months. A year later, I was exhausted from dealing with his inability to finish the house. There was no end in sight to the construction nightmare he had created. My energy was drained from the constant confrontations. I asked him to leave out of respect and honor for myself and to salvage my self-esteem.

"In everyone's life, at some time, our inner fire goes out. It is then burst into flame by an encounter with another human being. We should all be thankful for those people who rekindle the inner spirit."
— *Albert Schweitzer*

PowerSucking Parasites can be your greatest relationship lessons. They enter your life when your resistance is down and you may not see things objectively. When I was in my early thirties, I dated a man that I considered my true soul mate. It was less than a year after Hurricane Andrew. My soul mate came into my life and made me smile and laugh when circumstances were extremely serious for me.

What I did not then understand was that he suffered from a psychological disorder. When he was on, there was no keeping up with him. We traveled, went to concerts, movies, events and enjoyed each other's company. When he was off and in a depressed state, he barely acknowledged my existence. Of course, he barely acknowledged his own existence while he was in this condition. I remained in the relationship to support and help him. Just as I found myself drained of energy and ready to remove myself from the situation, he transformed back into his fun-loving self.

This was a man of great influence in the community. I was a young attorney recuperating from a devastating natural disaster. He promised to help me in my career and business transactions. It would have been easy for him to do so. Although he made promise after promise, he broke each one and never came through despite the fact that I continued to be there for him.

My energy was down and I was vulnerable. He was a parasite and sucked my energy for his benefit. His actions, however, taught me never to depend on anyone else to care for my business.

After my divorce, he contacted me and asked me to attend his birthday party. A little older and wiser, I accepted the invitation. During the course of the evening, I observed his behaviors as he attempted to treat me the same way that he treated me eleven years earlier. I was now a woman who had overcome serious challenges and adversity and was professionally accomplished. I was much stronger. I left, requesting that he never contact me again. I put an end, once and for all, to the PowerSucking parasitic relationship.

"There are "friends" who destroy each other,
but a real friend sticks closer than a brother."
—Proverbs 18:24 (NLT)

PowerSucking Parasites can also be members of your family. It has been said that you can choose your friends, but you can't choose your family. However, if your family members drain your energy and attempt to rob you of your power, you can create appropriate boundaries and choose not to allow them to affect you. It may be difficult to admit such things about people you love; however, the people closest to you are in an influential position to make adversity more challenging, guide you off purpose and sabotage your goals and dreams.

I love my brothers dearly; however, they are critical and controlling. They are PowerSucking Parasites. Their constant criticism and negativity towards me drains my energy and threatens my self-esteem. For example, when my father became ill, my brothers did little to assist in his care physically or financially. However, they judged and criticized me throughout my father's life for my involvement and participation. There was never any recognition from them for being there for my parents. My brothers never gave me credit for being able to juggle my personal and professional life with the care of our disabled father. There was never acknowledgement for anything I did for our parents. They did, however, repeatedly say and do hurtful things directed at me. I removed their negative influence from my life.

"If you are successful, you may win false friends and true enemies. Succeed anyway."
— *Mother Teresa*

In order to properly distinguish between Partners and Parasites, you must establish proper parameters and develop boundaries. If you were to make a circle, you would place the names of those people who are positive associations promoting progress on your path and purpose while protecting your personal empowerment within the boundary of the circle. The names of everyone else would be placed on the outside of the circle. Those people on the inside are your *PowerShift* Partners. Those on the outside are your PowerSucking Parasites.

This is not to say that you do not address those people that you have placed in your outer boundary. It does not mean that you do not speak to them or that you do not interact with them. It does mean, however, in order to protect your own energy, you only share your purpose, goals and dreams with the people within the inner boundary. You only trust and depend on those within your designated perimeter during a challenge or adversity in your life.

When you allow someone into your life and give them access to your purpose, goals and dreams, you're giving them access to the essence of your being. Stay within the positive perimeter. The area outside the perimeter is a toxic environment. It represents those persons for whatever reason may have negative energies and habits that are not in alignment with your purpose.

On your path to purpose and in mastering your goals and manifesting your dreams, you may have to leave people behind. It is difficult to acknowledge that some people are toxic for you. Take a moment and look at them as the gift of a mirror. They are showing you something that was lacking in yourself, something that you needed to develop. The continued development of self-confidence, self-esteem and self-worth, and the progress towards purpose, allows us to remove toxic people from our lives.

When you choose to stop the exchange of energy from someone on your outer boundary, I suggest that you do a meditation and exercise for release. Release these people with love in your silence and thank them for what they have brought into your life and taught you about yourself. Then let them go in love.

"The thief comes only to steal and kill and destroy;
I have come that they may have life,
and have it to the full."
— John 10:10 (NIV)

PowerShift Partners and PowerSucking Parasites exist in personal and professional relationships. They are defined in our environment as friends, family, parents, siblings, spouses, significant others, bosses, peers, employees, and teachers. They are anyone who has the ability to influence our power to face a challenge, master our goals and manifest our dreams. Ultimately, they are anyone who has the ability to influence our lives.

In celebrating the positive associations promoting progress on our path and purpose while protecting your personal empowerment we create a *PowerShift*!

> *PowerShift Reflection - In choosing a life in purpose, when facing adversity, mastering goals and manifesting dreams, we must be able to distinguish between the Partner and the Parasite. We can embrace those that fill our lives and being with positive energy and we can release those who attempt to engage us in negative energy. We must also remember that God has no boundaries and He is our first PowerShift Partner.*

CHAPTER
NINE

POWERSHIFT: FORGIVENESS

"May peace reign in the heart of every man and woman as they learn to accept and forgive each other in love."
— Mother Teresa

Living your life in purpose, mastering your goals and manifesting your dreams require that you be in a process of moving forward in your life. In order to advance through life's challenges, deal with adversity or progress through transitional periods you must also continue a forward motion. The momentum that drives you to your tomorrow takes the confidence and conviction to Shift your Power and let go and release your yesterday. This release is directed and driven by the *PowerShift* of Forgiveness.

Many times, in our hurt or anger, we have the human need to hold someone accountable for how we feel. We have a need to assign fault or make someone wrong in an effort to find closure. Whenever we place the responsibility for our feelings on someone or something else, however, we will never have closure. Forgiveness is the process of releasing feelings of resentment, hurt or anger which you hold against another person, event or thing. It is a place of peace where you no longer demand restitution, restoration, retribution or revenge. Forgiveness is the starting point where your joy can return.

Embracing our anger, resentments, hurt feelings, bitterness or ill will towards any person, event or thing relinquishes our personal power. Sadly enough, we surrender this power by blaming others for these hurts and pains whether or not the transgression was a real experience or simply some misperception. The symptoms manifesting in our physical body and mental thoughts are a product of a mind that cannot differentiate between offenses or events which were intentional, accidental, and circumstantial or created from the fallible thinking of a sensitive psyche. The outcome of this process can further develop into wounded self-esteem, a compromised immune system and blocked energies.

"To forgive is to set a prisoner free and discover that the prisoner was you."
— *Lewis B. Smedes*

The key to this fundamental *PowerShift* principle is that Forgiveness benefits the person doing the forgiving. The negative energy created by the absence of Forgiveness has the ability to affect our entire being by occupying our physical, spiritual and mental space. We can choose to reclaim our power and continue the forward motion in our lives once we have freed our mind and body and liberated ourselves from the hurt and pain, the desire for revenge or a need to prove who was right or wrong. We can create a *PowerShift* by engaging the power of Forgiveness.

"Forget the former things; do not dwell on the past."
— *Isaiah 43:18 (NIV)*

Forgiveness is a deliberate act of release on the part of the injured party. It is not dependent on the intention, remorse or repentance of the wrongdoer. It is a daring feat of the imagination that challenges you to conceive of a brighter future that is grounded in your blessings, gifts and talents. Forgiveness dares you to release the hurt and pain in order to regain your foothold on the path of your purpose, the mastery of your goals and the manifesting of your dreams. When you face adversity, it encourages you to give up the destructive thoughts about the situation and believe in the possibility of tomorrow's miracles. Forgiveness builds confidence that you can survive the pain and grow from it.

This *PowerShift* begins first with the realization that you have a choice to forgive. It is the conscious decision to release the negativity of the past, to acknowledge that your pain is not the final say in the matter and to move forward. In this decision, you reclaim your power by taking responsibility for yourself and allowing others to do the same.

"Then Peter came to him and asked, "Lord, how often should I forgive someone who sins against me? Seven times?" "No, not seven times," Jesus replied, "but seventy times seven."
— *Matthew 18:21-22 (NLT)*

While I was attending law school, I was engaged to be married to man whose background was different from my own. We grew up in different areas of the country, were raised with different levels of income, and were brought up in different faiths. We chose to respect each other's religious beliefs. During the development of our relationship, I found it enjoyable to share my traditions and beliefs and learn about his.

The wedding had been planned for the weeks after I completed my second year of law school. During my academic semester, I was busy between completing wedding details and preparing for my final exams. As with any wedding plans, a problem surfaced. This development did not concern the color of the bridesmaids' dresses or a misprint on the invitations. My fiancé's family refused to accept me because of my faith.

I was in the middle of wedding plans and in the middle of my semester. I did not have time to deal with this challenge and became frustrated for being rejected on the basis of my religion. The situation became even more serious when my future in-laws attempted to divide my fiancé and me by disowning him should he proceed with the marriage. It was working. I was deeply hurt by this lack of acceptance and resented being judged so unfairly.

My hurt turned into anger and further fueled the negativity surrounding the matter. One night, I had a dream where I was guided to a large book and given instructions to turn the pages. As I turned the pages, I looked at the words. I could not read or comprehend any of the lettering whatsoever. However, as I proceeded through the manuscript, the meaning of this dream became obvious. In turning the last page, I came across the word FORGIVE. There is nothing like a Divine cue card to shift your perspective on the situation.

Although it wasn't easy, I began to act from a position of Forgiveness towards my fiancé and his family. My confusion and contempt changed to compassion and I released my resentment. In the weeks that followed, my power returned and, shortly thereafter, I made the decision to break the engagement and call off the wedding.

Forgiveness allowed me to come from a place of personal strength, rather than from a position of compromised self-esteem. This release allowed me to make my choice to remove myself from a situation that was detrimental to my emotional well-being. I left a relationship that was not, ultimately, in my highest good. My Forgiveness was not dependent upon the remorse or apologies of my ex-fiancé's family. There was none. My Forgiveness of them did not depend upon them changing their attitude or opinion of the marriage. They would not. I am the one who made the conscious decision to change. I am the one who chose to release the past and proceed to a brighter future.

"The weak can never forgive. Forgiveness is the attribute of the strong."
— Mahatma Gandhi

Forgiveness can be the single most important process to restore health and harmony to our physical, spiritual and mental bodies. Maintaining a state of unforgiveness is unhealthy for the body, mind and soul. If bitterness, resentment and ill-will continue to pervade your emotional and spiritual being, you may lose your self-esteem or become as hurtful as the person who you perceive injured you. Choosing to remain in this state is choosing to remain a victim.

Lack of Forgiveness can drain your positive energy and wear you down physically. This state can contribute physiologically to such stress-related issues as ulcers, high blood pressure and fatigue. It can also exacerbate any other illnesses that your body may be fighting. It is human nature to replay a wounding event over in our minds, regardless of the damaging and destructive consequences. Our brain does not differentiate between long and short-term memory. Our mind does not know what is real or what is a figment of our imagination. In continuing to repeat these scenes, the same negative energy released throughout the physical body from the real event continues to be released again through each repeat performance. In other words, your mental matinee will cause the same physiological response.

"Forgetting what is behind and straining toward what is ahead, I press on toward the goal to win the prize for which God has called me."
— *Philippians 3:13-14 (NIV)*

There is nothing you can do to change yesterday. You do have power, however, over how you react and think about yesterday. You have the power over what is happening today. It is in what you choose to focus on and how you choose to respond in this present moment that determines the quality of your tomorrows. Your life follows your thoughts. Your life tomorrow will be the sum total of what you think today. Therefore, if you continue to focus on an offense and the person or event that caused it, you only perpetuate the problem and take it with you into your future. Another advantage to releasing your hurt and anger is that Forgiveness prevents past performance from affecting your future.

I met an artistically gifted man who was raised in the middle of the Depression. His father walked out on the entire family, leaving his mother as the only parent and provider for her three children. Throughout his life, this gentleman has carried a deep animosity towards his mother for his upbringing. Although he was never physically or mentally abused, in retrospect, he disagrees with many of her decisions. As an adult, he has chosen not to forgive her for the choices she made and the actions she took in her efforts to keep her children together.

Hindsight is 20/20. This man has manifested toxic emotions through the memories of his childhood. He further fuels the toxicity by replaying the events and speaking negatively about his parents. This poison has been the primary cause of the failure of his marriage and the ruin of his relationships with his children. His physical health is challenged, as well.

Regardless of how he was reared, and despite the overall environment the United States experienced as a result of the Depression, his choice not to forgive has allowed his past to dictate his present. His choice not to forgive may further destroy any happiness he could achieve in his future.

"I skate where the puck is going to be, not where it has been."
— *Wayne Gretzky*

Sports competitors know that looking back is a detriment to future performance. If you run track and field, the second it takes to look over your shoulder can cause you to knock down a hurdle or allow your opponent to pass you by. Golfers know that replaying a shot where the ball hit the rough or the water will land it there again.

In a jumping competition, horses and riders fly over fences competing against each other in an effort to beat the time clock. Every second counts and every rail down represents penalties against the competitors. If a horse tips or knocks a rail down as he sails over the jump, the rider does not have the luxury of looking over his or her shoulder. Instead, the horse and rider must stay focused on and prepare for the jumps in front of them.

In the same way, if we want to live an empowered life, we must refrain from looking back and lamenting over the downed rail of our past. If we don't, we fail to make the proper adjustments to insure our success in the opportunities ahead. Your point of power to create your future is in this present moment. Forgiveness brings you back to your point of power by releasing the past.

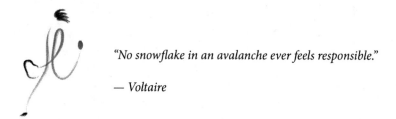

"No snowflake in an avalanche ever feels responsible."

— *Voltaire*

The process of Forgiveness also allows the lesson of the challenge or adversity to unfold. In a quiet meditative moment, you can ask the question, "What am I to learn from this?" Your answers may not come right away. However, any knowledge you gain can shift your perception and shift your energy. This shift will allow you to work within the situation more effectively. Change your perspective and accept the other person or event as a mirror to yourself. What were your strengths in the situation? What were your weaknesses? What issues prevented you from taking a different path? What were the lessons in this for other persons involved?

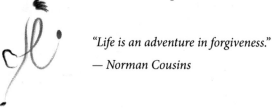

"Life is an adventure in forgiveness."

— *Norman Cousins*

If there are so many advantages to the *PowerShift* of Forgiveness, then why don't people forgive? There are several key reasons that keep people in a state of unforgiveness. The greatest misconception about Forgiveness is the internal belief system that equates forgiving with condoning. Forgiveness does not mean that you accept someone's behavior towards you or that you must overlook an egregious injury. Forgiveness takes you out of the role of victim and allows you to move beyond it.

I tell my clients that it takes GUTS to forgive. In other words, Give Up the Stuff! Let it go! Release it! Forgiveness is not excusing inappropriate behavior. Forgiveness is giving up all the things you want to hold on to in order to prove the principle of the matter. It is human nature to want to say, "I'm right, you're wrong!" To make matters even more complicated, we employ the outside influences of friends and family to come into agreement with our position.

The momentum may build and we can find ourselves in a desire for the other person to feel the pain that they inflicted on us. This is the next reason that people do not forgive. They want revenge! How many minutes have you wasted entertaining wild imaginings of getting even with someone who has caused you pain? It does not matter whether or not you would actually go through with it. This process amounts to nothing more that wasted mental energy and puts you on the same level as the person who hurt you. Give Up the Stuff and *Shift the Power*! Forgive and go forward!

Forgiveness also does not mean you have to reconcile with the person who caused the injury. For example, you can forgive a former spouse for his or her behavior during the marriage without having to ever come into contact with that person again. They do not need to request an apology for the benefits of Forgiveness to take effect. If an admission of guilt or a request for Forgiveness was required in order to experience the release, then selfish, hurtful people would be able to maintain their power over you for an indefinite period of time. No act of contrition on the part of the other person is necessary. Forgiveness is peace that does not depend on the actions of others. Forgiving benefits the forgiver and gives you the opportunity to create healthier, new relationships and situations.

"Forgiving does not erase the bitter past.
A healed memory is not a deleted memory.
Instead, forgiving what we cannot forget creates
a new way to remember. We change the memory
of our past into a hope for our future."
— Lewis B. Smedes

Another reason people choose not to forgive is to maintain their identity with the other person or event. The world is full of the walking-wounded who lug their luggage with them. Their scars are worn as badges of honor. To them, to forgive would mean to lose their individuality. They tell their story over and over again, re-opening the wounds each time. There is no such thing as a merry martyr. People in this state choose to remain trapped in a mental minefield awaiting the next explosion of emotions.

I shared with you earlier the story of the client that filed a lawsuit against a large retail store for an unsafe work environment. The damage to her was further perpetuated by the egregious actions of several of its employees. The events that took place in her life while she was employed with the company were disturbing and frightening. During the pendency of the suit, the client continued to relive the scenes over again for attorney interviews, depositions, trial preparation and finally trial.

Each time she gave her account of the story, the same anger, hurt and bitterness was present in her demeanor. She never made the choice to forgive. The case became the focal point of her life and became her identity. Her resentment and feelings of powerlessness were a catalyst to the downward spiral of eating disorders, alcoholism, drug abuse and abusive relationships. Five years from the date of filing, she had a verdict in her favor. However, the monies gained were modest in comparison to the price she paid in the years she lost remaining hurt, bitter and with little chance of rescuing her identity, self-esteem or life.

This is not to minimize the pain, wounds and scars of horrific offenses, or to diminish those people affected or disempowered by such acts in any way. However, failure to choose the freedom and empowerment of Forgiveness can imprison you in a pattern of destructive behaviors and demoralizing personal and professional relationships. If you continue to enter situations with this bitterness embedded in your mind and body, your lack of genuine self-worth can allow you to become the virtuous victim.

This mindset can keep you repeating the same cycle in different relationships and circumstances. Mere survival of the body and mind is death to the soul when you are disempowered. The chaos of the cycle continues. The definition of insanity is doing the same thing over and over, and expecting different results. In fully loving and forgiving yourself, you begin to break the stronghold of that cycle. In demonstrating Forgiveness for others, you can express the truth of your thoughts and emotions from a position of personal strength and empowerment. The decision to forgive is a powerful, conscious choice.

"When you hold resentment toward another, you are bound to that person or condition by an emotional link that is stronger than steel. Forgiveness is the only way to dissolve that link and get free."
— *Catherine Ponder*

Whom should we forgive? Being able to forgive and release past hurts is a critical tool for any relationship. This includes those relationships you want to maintain and those you want to move away from. The list includes, but is by no way limited to, parents, siblings, children, other family members, neighbors, bosses, employees, spouses, significant others, ex- spouses, former significant others, ex-fiancé's, friends, the guy who cut you off in traffic and the woman who took your parking space. The list is endless because it includes everyone in your life, or has ever been in your life, and anyone that you come into contact with.

I have also found that the *PowerShift* of Forgiveness and its release extends to events. Let's take, for example, natural disasters, such as Hurricanes Andrew, Charley or Katrina. Your home is damaged or fully destroyed. Your possessions have been damaged, swept away, or looted. No one is personally responsible. You were not personally targeted by the storms, although you may feel as if you were. You feel vulnerable, powerless and frightened. Many people will want to blame the government or the National Hurricane Center. The truth is they did not cause the event. Anger does not repair the damage to your house or to your soul.

I have shared with you my experiences of devastation with both Hurricanes Andrew and Charley. There was a phenomenon that occurred after Andrew. Like many others, I found myself waking up at 3:30 a.m. for months after the storm. This early morning hour represented the time that

Andrew's first bands of winds and rains made their terrifying entrance into Miami Dade County. Some might call it post-traumatic stress syndrome.

Although Charley hit Punta Gorda in the late afternoon, I again, began to wake up at 3:30 a.m. after the storm. Hurricane Charley caused me to relive the events that I had experienced twelve years earlier. I did not realize that I was harboring resentment and bitterness towards the storm. I knew that in order to survive the stress of Charley, I had to forgive Andrew.

We give these events names, and along with that name, we build personalities. Andrew took over two years of my life. He stole all my material possessions. He took my community. He robbed me of my security. Andrew violated me in a way that no other person or thing had ever done. With the impact of Charley, I now had two violators. I could choose to remain a victim of Andrew and allow him to dictate how I would recover from Charley. Or, I could forgive the storm and proceed with rebuilding my life once again.

I chose to forgive both Andrew and Charley. I became proactive in my release by giving workshops and seminars to service organizations and churches on how to recover from life- changing events. Andrew had made me an expert. In the meantime, when I released my feelings towards Andrew, I no longer woke up at 3:30 a.m.

Diseases and injuries must also be forgiven. People who overcome life-threatening illnesses or injuries share their experiences of forgiving their disease or injury in order to promote their health and well-being. Through the process of Forgiveness, you release it from your energy.

In my recovery from anorexia, I had to forgive the disease. I allowed this disorder to take five years of my life. The last of my teenage years and my early twenties were tossed into a dungeon of depression. Upon my recovery, I felt there was so much I had lost and so many things I had not fully experienced or enjoyed. Releasing the anger, and the bitterness of the years lost to the disease, helped me to move through my recovery.

Shortly thereafter, my father became brain-damaged. I was twenty-two years old and home from college when my father became sick with what we thought was a sinus infection and sore throat. He became non-responsive and I called 911.

Tests and scans revealed a dark mass on his brain that was thought to be an aneurysm. Subsequent emergency surgery revealed the presence of an infection on the brain. This was the beginning of a four month stay in intensive care and multiple surgeries. It was also a major transition in my life. My father survived the initial injury and subsequent surgeries. However, he was left with damage to his brain and was permanently disabled.

During the first weeks of his hospitalization, a family decision was made that I would manage the retail store owned by my parents. My mother was needed in the hospital and my brothers were married and employed. The store was out of town, so I withdrew from college and became a store manager.

Years later, I realized I had become angry and resentful on many levels towards that event and the subsequent decisions that were made. First, I was angry at my father's illness for taking the man that I knew as my father and shattering the security I had tried to re-establish after the anorexia. I was angry at my brothers for volunteering me to totally alter and interrupt the course of my life while theirs continued without being affected. My life, on the other hand, was affected drastically. I quit school and I ended a relationship that was heading towards marriage. I lost the opportunity to return to my riding coach. Years later when my brothers were critical of me, I relived this event and all the resentment and negative energy it carried.

"The depth of your compassion lies in your ability to forgive yourself."
— *Mark Graham*

I learned that there is another person on that list to forgive. It is the one you blame more than any other for things that go wrong in your day or life. This is the person you expect to support you on the path to your purpose, in mastering your goals and manifesting your dreams. This is the person in your life that handles all your challenges and adversities. This is the person you require the most from and can be disappointed the most by.

In order to go forward in purpose, face life's challenges and to achieve your goals and dreams, you must forgive yourself.

I was angry at myself because I lacked the strength to say "no" to decisions that were being made and affecting me. The focus, rightly so, was on my father's health. However, I had just recovered from anorexia and had not recovered sufficiently to have found my voice.

My anger and resentment of my father's illness did not surface until later in my life when there was a full, mature awareness of the course my life had taken as a result. In order to find balance and peace, I forgave the event, the illness and all the people who played a part in it. In order to restore my joy, I forgave myself.

"He who is devoid of the power to forgive, is devoid of the power to love."
— *Martin Luther King, Jr.*

How do you initiate the *PowerShift* of Forgiveness? How do you release the anger, resentment, bitterness and disappointment? It has already been stated that the first step is to make the conscious decision to forgive. This choice, itself, is significant progress. How many times though, have you tried to forgive someone only to find yourself replaying the injury and anger over again in your mind? Your decision has not been supported by a full release.

The negative emotions have the ability to affect our entire being. The negative energies we create can occupy our physical, spiritual, mental and emotional space. The act of Forgiveness should, therefore, incorporate the use of the body, mind and soul in order to fully release the injury, event or hurt.

The mind is supported in the release by making the conscious decision to forgive. Making this choice, however, may not be enough to overcome the images or the feelings that you want to replay in your mind. Visualization, therefore, is a key component to the release process. Sustain the act of Forgiveness by altering the images you see in your mind's eye. If you begin to replay the negative pictures, replace those images with calming, joy-filled scenes. Choose this scene ahead of time if you must. Make it your default setting.

In addition to visualizing an alternate picture in your mind, immediately say out loud, "Cancel." This directive supports the release from the mental and emotional body. Some physical act, such as one loud clap of your hands at the same time you say, "Cancel" or "Delete" interrupts of the flow of the past scenes and negative energy from your mental to your physical body.

Affirmations also strengthen your decision to forgive. Speak strong affirmative language and use words such as, "I choose to release this incident, to let it go and be free of it." You can use scriptures with or in place of affirmations if you so choose.

Do not continue to discuss the hurt and injury with others. Part of the processing of hurt and anger is discussing it with another. However, repeatedly bringing it into discussions further fuels the hurt and anger and prevents the injury from being released. If you need to talk about it, go to God.

Meditation will support the spirit and assist you in maintaining your conscious decision to forgive. I use simple crystal ball visualization during a Forgiveness meditation. As I enter a quiet space, I begin to breathe and relax. With each breath, I visualize light entering my body. This light forms a ball around my heart and I fill it with love. When the ball has fully developed and I feel the love emanating from it, I visualize the person I need to forgive. I then continue to visualize the ball of love and light as it leaves my heart and enters the heart of the person I am releasing and forgiving.

"You will know that forgiveness has begun when you recall those who hurt you and feel the power to wish them well."
— *Lewis B. Smedes*

Prayer supports the soul in the process of Forgiveness. If you find you cannot do it yourself, ask God for help. There was a person in my life who caused me great harm. I knew I needed to release him from my energy so I could be done with the negativity and move forward. It was extremely difficult for me to do so. I wanted to own my anger a bit longer, despite its destructiveness. I tried forgiving and supporting my decision with all the techniques outlined above, but I was not honoring my choice.

I went into prayer and asked for God's help in the matter. I tried the techniques again, and again, I found myself reliving all of the negative feelings. Several days later, when I was in prayer I acknowledged to God that I wasn't ready to forgive. I still hurt too much, so I placed the act of Forgiveness and my decision in God's hands. I placed the hurt in His hands, as well. I continued to use the techniques and each day the hurt subsided a little more. During this time, God showed me I was in a grieving process and needed to fully honor my grief and loss before I could honor my decision to forgive. Once I processed my grief and loss, I soon recalled the person and event without incurring any negative energy or thoughts about it.

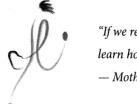

"If we really want to love we must learn how to forgive."
— *Mother Teresa*

In order to face life's challenges or adversities, or ease the course of transition, you must maintain forward motion in your life. This momentum also allows you to remain steadfast on your path of purpose, master your goals and manifest your dreams. The PowerShift of Forgiveness allows you to release the past injuries and hurts and to continue to advance in the direction of your destiny. Forgiveness takes inventory of your blessings and honors your talents and gifts by refusing to allow negative emotions and negative energy to obstruct their growth and development in your life. Forgiveness may not change the past, but it can alter your future. In forgiving, we create a PowerShift.

PowerShift Reflection - Forgiveness restores your mind, body and soul. It is a conscious decision to acknowledge the faith in yourself and re-establish confidence in your life. When we forgive, we surrender and give up yesterday's hurts and pain. Through this release we recognize our significance and celebrate our tomorrows.

CHAPTER
ᴢɛᴨ

POWERSHIFT: GRATITUDE

"Gratitude bestows reverence, allowing us to encounter everyday epiphanies, those transcendent moments of awe that change forever how we experience the world."
— *John Milton*

The *PowerShift* of Gratitude is put into action by the statement of two simple words: Thank you! In its simplicity, Gratitude improves everything in your life. It is a powerful spiritual tool that can positively affect your health, relationships, abundance and overall quality of life. Whatever it may be that you desire to create, Gratitude is the medium that puts the energy into motion.

Coming from a mood of Gratitude acknowledges your blessings, talents and gifts from the Divine and opens you to receive more in your life. When Gratitude shifts your focus to your blessings, your thoughts shift away from lack. When Gratitude shifts your focus to what is right with your life, your thoughts cannot be on what is going wrong. When Gratitude shifts your focus to your purpose, goals and dreams, your thoughts cannot be on fear and failure.

Gratitude also makes you more resilient in facing challenges, adversities and in going through life's transitions. Your life is enriched through this practice, regardless of the circumstances in which you may find yourself. Gratitude allows you the opportunity to live in a positive mental state despite what may appear in the physical world. It can support your inner strength by enhancing your mental and physical energies. Gratitude decreases the resistance of fear and anxiety and increases your ability to survive and thrive. A mood of Gratitude gives you the ability to create positive outcomes from negative situations.

Maria had been employed by the same company for fifteen years when it closed. Although she had a good resume and extensive experience, job interviews produced no productive leads for employment. Negative emotions could have prevailed; however, Maria chose to remain in Gratitude. She was grateful for the length of time she was employed, the contacts she made at the company and the experience she received at her position. Maria also expressed Gratitude for a new opportunity, although it had not manifested.

Making the most of a challenging situation, she accepted a lower-paying position that was not in alignment with her experience. She remained in a mood of Gratitude at her new job. Two months later, a client of her previous employer saw Maria at lunch and inquired where she was employed. Realizing that she was working beneath her professional capabilities, the client informed Maria of a job opening in his office. Knowing that she was well-qualified, he assured her that he would give her a good recommendation. Maria applied for and got the job. She remained in Gratitude throughout her employment situation. Although she had accepted a lesser paying job, the position placed her in an environment where an opportunity presented itself. Maria's mood of Gratitude enabled her to work through a negative situation to a positive outcome.

A mood of Gratitude also expands exponentially. When you start practicing Gratitude, it reminds you that you have all you need and it will show you that you have even more for which to be thankful. Giving thanks refocuses your mind towards confidence and optimism. Gratitude offers a renewed sense of clarity of purpose as it clears out the negative energies that block your good from coming to you.

The Shift of Power emanates from the change in the mental, physical and spiritual energies produced when your thoughts are those of appreciation. The change in your mental energies occurs when your mind acknowledges those things, situations and people who support you in some way. Your physical body responds and you experience reduced anxiety and a sense of overall well-being. The shift in the spiritual energies occurs as Gratitude aligns you with God and your inner-resources. When you engage the *PowerShift* of Gratitude, your heart and soul are filled with love. Resentment, anger, fear and selfishness cannot survive in its presence. The soul and spirit re-enters its familiar state.

"To speak gratitude is courteous and pleasant, to enact gratitude is generous and noble, but to live gratitude is to touch Heaven."
— *Johannes A. Gaertner*

THREE LEVELS OF GRATITUDE

1) **EXPRESSING GRATEFULNESS FOR AN IMMEDIATE ACT OR DEED**

2) **STATE OF MIND OF BEING GRATEFUL**

3) **UNCONDITIONAL GRATEFULNESS**

Gratitude is a practice. It is a complete acknowledgement of all that is right. You can think of Gratitude as existing on three different levels. Level one is simply a feeling of being thankful. This feeling exists solely on the emotional level and is expressed in the physical world by saying, "Thank you." This level of Gratitude is typically an immediate response for an act or deed performed for your benefit, or for some material thing which you have requested or for which you have worked.

The second level of Gratitude graduates from a feeling to a state of being. It is the condition of being thankful. This level of Gratitude is more than a reaction or a physical expression. It exists on the mental plane and is a state of mind rather than a brief, passing emotion.

In terms of creating the *PowerShift*, the first two levels of Gratitude only touch the surface as an underlying attitude and physical expression. For example, you are in a restaurant and your waiter brings you a cup of coffee that you requested. You say, "Thank you." This is level one. Level two is physically expressing your appreciation, as well as acknowledging the good service you have been shown. The coffee you requested and received is the emotion. The recognition of the coffee, as representative of the overall excellent service is the condition of the mind.

The third level of Gratitude transforms your focus. You are grateful for your life's journey regardless of your circumstances. When Gratitude becomes unconditional, the state of your entire life develops to keep in stride. This level is when you go from level one, appreciating the cup of coffee and the good service, to level two, acknowledging the collective circumstances it took to get you into the restaurant at that specific place and time. Level three is honoring the global effort it took to place that cup of coffee on your table. This level of Gratitude is not diminished by life's challenges, such as when the waiter spills the coffee in your lap!

Level three is not a temporary state. It exists on the spiritual plane and serves as a connection to God. At this level, Gratitude unites the mind, body and soul to manifest your thoughts into reality. It is the appreciation, not only for your health, well-being and material possessions, but also for the lessons learned that have developed you into the person you are at this moment.

"This is the day the Lord has made.
We will rejoice and be glad in it."
— *Psalm 118:24 (NLT)*

Dare to imagine your life as you choose to wake up every morning in joy, peace and appreciation of the day ahead! This is where the practice of Gratitude must begin. If you desire to live in purpose, master your goals and manifest your dreams you must begin with a mood of Gratitude. Creating financial prosperity, as well as healthy personal and professional relationships, must start with a mood of Gratitude. If you are facing life's challenges or going through a transition, you must maintain a mood of Gratitude to find your inner peace and power.

What type of Gratitude would you feel if you were living the life of your dreams? Challenge yourself to create the appreciation for that life now, even in the most unlikely circumstances. You will notice that you begin to attract the relationships, opportunities and resources that resonate with the Gratitude. The mood of Gratitude is the backdrop on which you can set your stage for life. Universal energies will support you in your endeavors and allow you to experience a deeper connection to God. Remember, being grateful for the life you create now, before it manifests in the physical world, attracts the circumstances congruent with that Gratitude.

A mood of Gratitude is a continual presence of appreciation and gratefulness. Some people only feel grateful when something great happens to them or they receive a gift. When you live energized with Gratitude, you will give thanks for anything or anyone who has benefited you, whether they meant to or not. When you are charged with the power of Gratitude, you just give thanks, period.

A mood of Gratitude is the acknowledgement that God is the creator of all things. It is the understanding that our independence is an illusion and by releasing this illusion we fully accept and appreciate the Creator and His creation. It is the recognition of the simple acts and activities we once took for granted. The mood of Gratitude is appreciating the ability to breathe the air, knowing that there are those who would welcome the opportunity to breathe without being attached to a canister of oxygen. It the appreciation of standing on your own two feet, knowing there are those who would welcome the opportunity to get out of a wheelchair and walk from the last parking space in the lot.

A mood of Gratitude is a choice. It is not dependent on things over which we have no control or the present circumstances in our lives. Gratitude enables us to accept both our victories and challenges with the same appreciation and graciousness.

"If you don't like something, change it. If you cannot change it, change your attitude. Don't complain."
— *Maya Angelou*

There are two main obstacles to developing and maintaining a mood of Gratitude. Although they may not seem like major blockages, they have the ability to inhibit the work of this *PowerShift* in your life. The first obstacle is complaining. Complaining is the direct opposite of Gratitude. Gratitude is energy of power and inner-strength. Complaining is an energy of disempowerment or weakness. Gratitude is energy of abundance. Complaining is an energy of lack. Gratitude is energy of achievement. Complaining is an energy of disappointment.

There is no positive purpose to complaining. Practicing Gratitude is transformative and can change the way we view our world. Gratitude affirms the positive. Complaining is also transformative. Complaining affirms the negative. It is just as easy to act from a position of Gratitude as it is to engage in complaining. More often than not, however, we choose to deplete the energy of our positive emotions and optimistic outlook by complaining. Complaining creates fear, resentment, jealousy, anxiety, anger and self-loathing. It weakens your connection to God by creating the wrong focus and allowing your mind to remain preoccupied with your problems. Continuous complaining can lead to feelings of despair and victimization.

What do we have to complain about? Our jobs. Not having enough money. Our spouses. Our kids. Lack of appreciation. Our political leaders. We are not happy, and we complain. Or, could it be that we complain and then we are not happy? As we have discussed in previous chapters, what you think about will increase, and what you focus on expands. It is necessary to Shift your Power from problems and negativity in order to experience the joy and positive energies of life.

Of course, it is important to give some attention to life's problems and challenges in order to process and manage them. The key to doing so is to minimize the attention and energy on the problem and maximize your focus on what is right. Focusing on the wrong areas may undermine Gratitude and cause you to overlook and take for granted all the things, people and situations which support you on a daily basis.

For instance, focusing so heavily on what is lacking, or what we do not like about our lives, keeps us from paying attention to the good in the situation that counterbalances them. We don't like our job; however, we do have a job and it pays the bills, provides for the family or allows us to take a vacation. Be grateful! We don't have enough money; however, we live in a country where we can create opportunities to make more money, or there may be assistance if we go through significant financial challenges. Be grateful! We want our spouse to change; however, we have the option to love and accept this person and our commitment or to legally dissolve the relationship. Be grateful! We complain about others not appreciating us; however, there are those people who love and support us on a daily basis. Be grateful! We complain about our political leaders; however, we live in a country where we can remove our leaders from office and elect new people without the fear of retribution. Be grateful!

"Feeling grateful or appreciative of someone or something in your life actually attracts more of the things that you appreciate and value into your life."
— *Christiane Northrup*

The second obstacle to establishing a mood of Gratitude is the fear that if you are grateful despite your present circumstances, you may relinquish your goals and dreams and settle for where you are and what you have at the present moment. Your thoughts may say something to the effect, "Well, what I have now is okay. I have to be grateful for what I have. I am better off than some, so I will be happy with where I am and what I've got." This is not true Gratitude; rather, it is a forced effort of complacency.

In the intensity to achieve goals and advance in the workforce, there is an assumption that practicing Gratitude makes you appear weak in the wake of professional competition. Some believe it is a sign of acceptance of circumstances and situations with no drive to do or be anything more.

Gratitude is proactive. By fully appreciating what you have achieved, you increase your abilities and opportunities for achieving and receiving more. Gratitude does not reduce your drive. It increases your motivation and determination. The true practice of Gratitude demonstrates that you are prepared to live in purpose, master your goals and manifest your dreams. As you develop the practice of Gratitude, you become the person that leads the life you have always known you were destined to live.

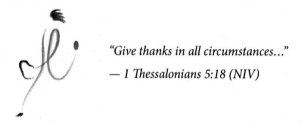

"Give thanks in all circumstances..."
— *1 Thessalonians 5:18 (NIV)*

"Give thanks in all circumstances." This statement embodies the true practice of Gratitude. Despite the situation in which you find yourself, regardless of the hurt and pain you have suffered, and even though you may have incurred extraordinary losses, you *Shift the Power* and practice Gratitude.

Gratitude is the key to making it through the adversities and challenges we face and promotes the healing process that takes place afterwards. There is suffering, hurt and pain. Decide where you want to direct your focus. Do you see yourself as a victim? Or do you view yourself as a person who is strong and capable? Choose the frame of mind in which you will place your future.

This concept of Gratitude may appear unrealistic to you. Perhaps you are going through or recently went through something that caused you pain. You may still be so consumed with the hurt and loss that you see no reason to be thankful. It has been my experience through the challenges and adversity that I have faced, that my ultimate success can be attributed to Gratitude.

How can you be practice Gratitude and be grateful in all circumstances? I had just graduated from law school, passed the bar exam and was scheduled to open my office on August 24th, 1992, the exact date Hurricane Andrew devastated Homestead, Florida. This devastating event was not on my schedule or agenda!

I remember those hours when Andrew made landfall. I was staying at my former home, assisting a friend with his kennel. The hurricane was supposed to come in North Dade. Miami Beach had been evacuated. The kennel was filled with dogs whose owners left the area or were staying at shelters that were not pet-friendly.

Hurricanes do not always do what they are forecasted to do and Andrew veered south. I heard the tornadoes touch down around the house. Even in the darkness, I saw shadows flying past the windows and striking the outside walls. I heard a window blow out in one of the rooms where the dogs were housed. Then silence. We could not check on the dogs for fear of causing more damage to the structure from the winds blowing through the opening. We could only reinforce the door and stay where we were.

Andrew continued through the southern tip of Florida and proceeded to head through the Everglades. When the winds died down and the pressure neutralized in the dogs' room, we opened the door to find all of the animals safe. I walked outside and caught my first glimpse of the storm's destruction. Not a tree stood upright. The horses' barn was nothing more than a pad and footers.

I attempted to make it back to the house that my parents and I owned. My parents had stayed with friends five miles north and I did not know how their house had endured the high winds and tornadoes. I prayed that we would meet up soon. During the trip, I found the one pay phone still standing and, as I said before, made the only call to find out that my horses were safe.

At last, I arrived at our property. Our house was leveled and what remained was scattered all across the premises. At the time of the storm, we were in the process of building. Our insurance coverage was negligible compared to the significant losses. We would have little money to rebuild.

The first day ended. There was only darkness. The air was hot and muggy. Still in shock, I awoke as the sun rose on the second day with no running water, electricity or flushing toilets. The gravity of the situation and the significance of the devastation set in as I realized the previous day had not been a bad dream after all.

The next two years were a journey of rebuilding a house and a life. I lost everything I owned and suffered a substantial setback professionally. I had no job and no legal practice. Like many Floridians, my parents and I were cheated financially by workers who were supposed to be helping hurricane victims. Within the year, what we had recouped materially was stolen from us by a person who had worked on the house.

How can you practice Gratitude in this situation? If I had not found things for which to be grateful, I would not have emotionally or physically survived. If I had not found things for which to be grateful, I would not have healed.

I made a Gratitude list:

- **I was grateful that my parents and I made it through the storm without injury.**
- **I was grateful that my horses were not in the county at the time. Many animals were killed and many others had to be destroyed as a result of their injuries.**
- **I was grateful that the house that I was in during the storm was protected and withstood the tornadoes that circulated around it. Studies indicated that 75 tornadoes touched down in the two square mile area between the house I owned and the one I stayed in.**
- **I was grateful that the dogs being boarded in the kennel were safe after the window blew out and compromised the integrity of the structure.**
- **I was grateful for the working pay phone where I made my call to check on my horses.**
- **I was grateful to the people who came to our aid from across the country.**
- **I was grateful to the volunteers from the service organizations and churches that helped us rebuild.**

- I was grateful for all of the workers who left their families and came to clear the roads and replace the power and telephone lines.
- I was grateful to FEMA who supplied us with a mobile home on the property while we rebuilt.
- I was grateful to the members of our armed forces and police forces who patrolled the area and kept us safe.
- I was grateful to neighbors who left bread at the gate when they had received an extra loaf.
- I was grateful for friends who sent me clothes.
- I was grateful for the kindness of strangers who sent the necessities of life such as toothbrushes, toothpaste, toilet paper and sunscreen.
- I was grateful for the food and ice.
- I was grateful for the lessons learned and the strength I found within myself to endure.
- I was grateful to God for His guidance, love and protection throughout.

The Gratitude did not end upon moving back into the house. To this day, I am grateful to pay my electric bill and for a simple cup of ice. I also continue to be grateful that I became a more sympathetic and understanding person for the experiences I endured and that those lessons carried through in my professional life.

In the midst of the unimaginable, if you are not living in Gratitude, then you are accepting the wounds being inflicted upon you and choosing to remain a victim of your circumstances. You are choosing to let negative energies decide and dictate your future. Don't misunderstand me. I am a normal human being. Many days I cried. There were moments when I screamed. Sometimes I wondered if God had forgotten about me. At times, I felt angry, frustrated and exhausted. The key is that I didn't remain in that state of emotion. I practiced Gratitude in order to survive the challenging events that tried to define my life. In the most horrific circumstances, the only way that I navigated my way through the turmoil-mentally, physically and spiritually-was to be thankful for all that was good. And there was good.

"If you concentrate on finding whatever is good in every situation, you will discover that your life will suddenly be filled with gratitude, a feeling that nurtures the soul."

— *Rabbi Harold Kushner*

Gratitude is the refractor that shifts the focus of the lens through which you view your life. Your glasses do not have to be rose-colored to acknowledge the beauty of the rose, rather than the pain inflicted by the thorns. However, many of us focus on the deficiencies in our lives, and barely perceive the good that counterbalances them.

My father was not a demonstrative man and he had difficulty showing affection. I am sure that much of his inability to express love was due to the environment in which he was raised. I knew that my father loved me as a child; however, there was not a great deal of emotional or physical support.

Along with my mother, I spent 23 years as my father's caretaker. As he grew older, my father became more aware of my life choices with regards to his illness. Professionally, I remained a sole-practitioner, rather than working for another law firm. This allowed me to dictate my own schedule and be available for my father's doctor's appointments and hospital stays, as well as his day to day needs. Personally, my dating options were limited and, therefore, my choice to have a family was also hindered. In his later years, my father was appreciative of my presence in his life. We became much closer than we ever were when I was growing up.

When I became an attorney, the lessons I learned from dealing with my father's health issues and disabilities gave me more strength and compassion with my clients. The experience of being a long-term caretaker made me a better person, as well as a better attorney.

It was not until later in life that I realized that my father's illness had affected many aspects of my personal and professional decisions. If I focused on what I missed, such as raising children or the opportunity to make partner in a firm, then I would overlook the good that came out of the challenge of his disabilities. I was grateful for the lessons I learned, the strength I found and for the person I became. I was grateful for the relationship that I developed with my father through his illness. What could be viewed as a curse on my life can also be seen as a blessing. What could be viewed as an obstacle can also become the gift.

"If someone has enough money to live well and sees a brother or sister in need but shows no compassion— how can God's love be in that person? Dear children, let's not merely say that we love each other; let us show the truth by our actions."
— *1 John 3:17-18 (NLT)*

When your practice of Gratitude develops to where you no longer focus on your problems, your heart opens to the problems of others. When your practice of Gratitude develops to where you acknowledge your blessings, then your focus shifts to sharing gifts with others. This is what I call the Gift Shift. It is the natural extension of the practice of Gratitude.

Gift Shifting is the recognition of your blessings and gifts and using them to meet the needs of others. It can be as simple as acknowledging the Gratitude of your beautiful day by offering a smile to a stranger. Or, in recognizing the abundance that is in your life, leaving an extra tip to a waiter or waitress who is struggling as a single parent or trying to buy school books. Gift Shifting can celebrate your family and friends by a visit to a lonely resident in a nursing home. It can be part of an organized charity, such as serving food in the homeless shelter or helping to rebuild a devastated community. The cost of the gift you give is unimportant. What you receive in return cannot be measured by a dollar amount. It is the feeling that the gift creates within you and the energy it sends out to others, that is significant.

I had the opportunity to witness a Gift Shift and be the recipient of the energy it created while flying home from a business trip. As I boarded the plane and located my seat in coach, I noticed a woman in fatigues. Prior to take-off, she was introduced by the flight attendant. The officer had served three tours of duty in Iraq and was on her way home for leave. The passengers on the plane gave her an appreciative round of applause.

When the flight landed, the flight attendant again thanked the officer for her service to us. She also thanked the gentleman who gave up his seat in first class to the officer. This is the true essence of Gratitude and the Gift Shift. This man acknowledged his blessings and showed appreciation to a person who was away from her family and willing to give her life to protect us. Although the officer was the recipient of the Gift Shift, each member of that flight had the ability to experience it as well. I was touched and filled with pride for our military personnel, and the respect and appreciation for the simple gesture.

"To be able to give away riches is mandatory if you wish to possess them. This is the only way that you will be truly rich."
— *Muhammad Ali*

Some people in our society live only for themselves. They have no desire to assist anyone in need or to even know that a need exists. They have no motivation to promote someone in their endeavors. They fear that if they help another, it will diminish their financial statement or their standing in the workplace or community. This behavior is contrary to spiritual principles. People who engage in this type of behavior will find it difficult to be happy or satisfied in their lives. The acquisition of material possessions or professional standing will never provide them with true satisfaction. They will constantly search for more to satisfy their desires for wealth, power or security. More will constantly elude them.

"Give and you will receive. Your gift will return to you in full—pressed down, shaken together to make room for more, running over, and poured into your lap. The amount you give will determine the amount you get back."
—Luke 6:38 (NLT)

Gratitude cannot coexist with selfishness. Gift Shifting helps you to develop and acknowledge a sense of abundance in your life. You give from an infinite supply and you know that you have more than enough. You also know that in helping someone else, you have actually helped yourself.

Giving to others who have served you well, been affected by circumstances similar to yours in the past, or who are disadvantaged physically, mentally or financially, emphasizes the gifts and blessings that are evident in your own life. By demonstrating to God that you are willing to give away a part of you, the doors open to receive even greater things.

Immediately after Hurricane Andrew, I experienced a Gift Shift. I mentioned previously that the first carloads of volunteers came from South Carolina. Banners attached to their cars read, "They helped us with Hugo, let's help them with Andrew." The smallest gifts from a cup of cold water to a bar of soap were the greatest treasures amidst the catastrophe. The material object was not the only part of the gift. It was the fact that someone cared enough and was thankful enough for their own well-being to reach out and give.

Since Andrew and Charley, I have shifted that gift to other areas. I personally can no longer watch areas devastated by storms, wildfires, earthquakes, tornadoes or other natural events without empathizing with their situation and life circumstances. I donate money and goods to those affected and do so in Gratitude for my well-being. I recognize my blessings and honor those people who were there for me in my time of need.

The greatest good you can do for another is not just to share your riches but to reveal to him his own."
— Benjamin Disraeli

We were created to give. Our soul is energized and thrives when we participate in this spiritual principle. Your talents and abilities are God-given gifts and resources. Shifting your Power to the needs and wants of others will allow you to experience more of those Divine gifts. You are more likely to live in purpose, master your own goals and manifest your dreams when you assist others in doing the same.

I have a close friend that came to this country from China at the age of fifteen. Upon her arrival, Barbara worked in fields in Miami, Florida, picking vegetables with the migrant workers. At the age of sixteen, she got married, and at seventeen, she welcomed the birth of her daughter. Barbara later divorced her husband and, as a single mother, raised her child in a country that was still foreign to her.

Barbara's entrepreneurial spirit and great determination carried her from vegetable picking to owning her own business. Her daughter, whom she put through college, is now excelling in her own professional endeavors. Barbara acknowledges that she had help on her journey and she remains grateful to those who extended themselves on her behalf.

Barbara's practice of Gratitude extends to Gift Shifting. She recognizes her gifts and blessings by supporting others in realizing their dreams. Barbara has financially assisted others, in personal, professional or academic pursuits, who played an integral part in her daughter's life and initiation into American culture. Barbara gave her daughter her foundation in eastern philosophy and traditions from her native country. She appreciates the people who influenced her daughter and introduced her to western culture. In her support, with both financial contributions and emotional encouragement, Barbara reveals to others their talents and gifts.

"Let no one ever come to you without leaving better and happier. Be the living expression of God's kindness: Kindness in your face, kindness in your eyes, kindness in your smile."

— *Mother Teresa*

Barbara also spends part of her weekends at nursing homes. She visits the parents of friends who have passed on. These elderly people have no other family or friends and Barbara gives her time to share conversation and a meal. Her Gift Shift to them is a link to the memory of their departed child.

I have personally experienced Barbara's Gift Shift. In the course of the day, I have many demands placed on my time and energies. It is part of my job to solve other people's problems. Many times, I do so at the expense of my own needs. On the way home from work I have stopped at Barbara's business to take a few minutes and catch up. She encourages me to sit and relax, and serves me a cup of hot tea and a snack. It is a relaxing moment in an otherwise tiring workday and the tea and her caring hospitality are truly gifts for me.

"We make a living by what we get, but we make a life by what we give."

— *Winston Churchill*

You may not realize you have been a Gift Shift recipient until many years have passed. My grandmother lived in a small town in Alabama and raised three children on her own during the Great Depression. My grandfather left them all and relatives tried to convince my grandmother to place her children in an orphanage. She refused to do so and raised them alone without the social or government benefits that we have access to today.

During World War I, my grandmother worked in the cotton mill in Alabama. She worked with the looms which ran 24 hours a day. My grandmother wasn't permitted to leave the loom after her shift was over until the next person showed up to relieve her. Many days, she worked past her designated time, waiting for a relief employee. My grandmother never left the mill until her hair was brushed clean and her clothes were changed. Money was tight, but she found the time and resources to bake cakes and pies for her children and their friends. Despite the challenges and adversity, she created a home for her children.

My grandmother was an amazing woman and I have benefitted from her Gift Shift of strength, determination and love. I am grateful for the gift of her family values and the importance she placed on raising her children, regardless of the hardships she encountered. She left these resources as a legacy to the generations that succeeded her.

My grandmother loved animals and this was another gift she gave to her children and grandchildren. She also enjoyed feeding the birds and squirrels and watching them play in the yard. I didn't appreciate the joy she experienced from this until several years after her passing.

One day, I put a small bird feeder in a tree and threw out some seed. Each day the amount of the seed increased as the numbers of birds multiplied. I attracted blue jays, cardinals, doves, woodpeckers and a whole array of birds I cannot name. I enjoyed watching them fly in, interact, scarf up the seed and play in the bird bath. I know that my grandmother was watching. I could almost hear her giggle when the woodpecker continued to peck on my house, knowing I would come out and throw more peanuts.

The joy I receive from this is a Gift Shift from my grandmother for which I am grateful. Each morning, I think about her as I fill the feeders and watch the birds for a few quiet moments while I sip my morning coffee. My actions keep my grandmother close. It is my way of honoring her and showing my Gratitude for all the gifts she gave to me.

"We have one life; it soon will be past; what we do for God is all that will last."

— *Muhammad Ali*

Gratitude is the energy-generating and joy-filling *PowerShift*. Its energy has the ability to see you through challenges and adversity, steady your path on purpose, master your goals and manifest your dreams! When you are in a mood of Gratitude, you have created a *PowerShift*!

PowerShift Reflection - Choose to live every day in a mood of Gratitude. Where there is Gratitude, there is an absence of fear, resentment and despair. Your heart is open and you are connected to God and the Divine dimension of the world. When you acknowledge your blessings, you acknowledge your greatness and significance.

CHAPTER
ELEVEN

THE EMPOWERSHIFTED LIFE

"Sometimes it's important to work for that pot of gold. But other times it's essential to take time off and to make sure that your most important decision in the day simply consists of choosing which color to slide down on the rainbow."

— *Douglas Pagels*

Life is meant to be enjoyed, not just endured. Each day offers a new opportunity, an uncharted path or an exciting adventure. We were not designed to merely exist. We are destined to embrace, engage and celebrate our lives. Adversity and dreams are indicators of our purpose. However, if we get consumed by life's challenges or obsessed with mastering our goals, we may fail to remember that each moment is a gift. We are not guaranteed the next.

PowerShift Reflection – I cherish my life for the blessing that it is each and every day!

There is no doubt that we will face day-to-day disappointments and delays. Many of us will experience great loss from transitions, challenges and adversity. Most of the hardships will be caused by unforeseen happenings that do not give advance warning of their arrival or allow us the benefit of preparation. The form of the challenge may vary for each of us - a natural disaster, the loss of a loved one, a pink slip on the job or a serious illness or injury – but the results may be similar. Physical, financial and emotional setbacks may open the door for despair, distress and depression. Empowering yourself by accessing the eight PowerShifts - Purpose,

Prayer, Divine Direction, Time and Focus, Words and Thoughts, Partners, Forgiveness, Gratitude - will keep goals and dreams from getting lost in the underlying current of chaos and confusion.

PowerShift Reflection - I see and experience the rainbow through the darkness of the storm!

THE POWERSHIFTS

- **PURPOSE**

- **PRAYER**

- **DIVINE DIRECTION**

- **TIME AND FOCUS**

- **WORDS AND THOUGHTS**

- **PARTNERS**

- **FORGIVENESS**

- **GRATITUDE**

You may have no fault or control in the events that change the course of your life. However, you can always control how you choose to define the events in your life. Transitions can be a life-changing transformation or a tweak in the path of your purpose. Challenges can be fortuitous experiences that empower you to master your goals. Adversity can serve as a course-correction encouraging you to access and manifest your dreams.

PowerShift Reflection – I have the authority to define and direct my experience!

Goals and dreams hold challenges of their own. Positive experiences such as getting a promotion or finding Mr. or Ms. Right can present you with challenges, as well. For example, a new position brings new responsibilities and sometimes new headaches, and a new love interest poses the challenge of having to compromise with another person when you're used to doing things your way.

You will also make your fair share of mistakes on the path to your purpose, goals and dreams. We do not live in a perfect world where everything goes according to plan. It is how you are able to redefine, redirect and refocus that will determine your successes in life. PowerShift Reflection – I have the ability to navigate my path to purpose, master my goals and manifest my dreams!

"It is within my power either to serve God or not to serve Him. Serving Him, I add to my own good and the good of the whole world. Not serving Him, I forfeit my own good and deprive the world of the good, which was in my power to create."

—Leo Tolstoy

Challenges are the perfect time to re-create your life because they force you out of your comfort zone. Most people will stay in their comfort zone because although there's not a lot of pleasure, there's not a lot of pain either. However, when you get uncomfortable, you find that you have resources, gifts and talents that you haven't even tapped. During times of challenge, you have the ideal opportunity to use these resources to turn the events around and create the life you truly want to live. You have the chance to share your gifts and talents on a greater level. Use the PowerShifts to keep your purpose, dreams and goals in front of you. Allow their energy to motivate and encourage you to work through any adversity or challenge. The PowerShifts make you aware that what you are doing in life is more significant than the situation at hand.

PowerShift Reflection – I have the confidence to step out of my comfort zone and create the life I want to live!

"When one door closes, another opens. But we often look so regretfully upon the closed door that we don't see the one that has opened for us."
— Alexander Graham Bell

If we desire to turn adversity into something good in our lives, then we must respond rather than react. Blaming and wallowing in self-pity are not productive responses. They are based on resistance and fear and place us in the position of reacting to our environment. When we respond correctly—by trusting God and empowering ourselves—we are then able to direct the situation and reap the benefits to master our goals and manifest our dreams.

PowerShift Reflection – I live in purpose and lead an EmPower-Shifted Life!

The PowerShifts energize you emotionally, mentally and spiritually. Fully embracing the EmPowerShifted life means that you make the energy of the PowerShifts a part of your daily routine. The EmPowerShifted life calls on you to engage in self-care as well. We have been conditioned to believe that success is achieved through being busy. Productivity is measured by activity. More meetings and more demands is equated with more power. In the workplace and home, multitasking is common and managing stress is a normal state of being. When we are meeting needs and deadlines or managing adversity and goals, the first thing we often fail to do is to take time to restore our joy and peace. We fail to take time for ourselves.

Self-nurturing can be stressful. It is often easier to care for another or fully focus on a goal or challenge than it is to see to our own needs. It takes physical energy to navigate adversity, traverse life's transitions, master goals and manifest dreams. Self-care is required in order for the PowerShifts to function in your life at maximum efficiency.

We are the custodians of our body. As the guardians of our physical well-being, our requirements of proper nutrition, sufficient sleep and adequate exercise should be of paramount importance. However, when we are overcommitted or overwhelmed we sometimes consider those requirements luxuries. Our sleep may be interrupted. Our diet may consist of empty calories that feed our time frame rather than our bodies. Drive-through windows and fast-food become a mainstay of our dietary sustenance. Or, we may skip meals altogether. Caffeine may be used as a nutritional supplement to make it through the end of the day. Exercise becomes something we will start "tomorrow."

It can become an endless cycle. Positive and negative stress can cause you to lose sleep. You reach for caffeine because you are tired and lack physical energy and mental sharpness. Trying to save time, you grab a candy bar or stop at a fast-food restaurant. Lacking adequate sleep, hydration and nutrition, places your body under more stress.

You are more likely to become depressed, fatigued and anxiety ridden when you're engaging in negative physical habits. In this physical state, challenges become more challenging, goals become more exhausting and dreams feel as if they will never come true. It becomes more difficult to engage the full force of the PowerShifts when the needs of the physical body are ignored.

We need to live our lives so as not to damage our bodies. Staying in stress serves no purpose. It will hinder you as you manifest your dreams or navigate through transitions and challenges. Stress will rob you of your joy, peace and happiness. In fully embracing the EmPowerShifted life, you pursue the pot of gold that you determine to be your goals and dreams. You are also inspired to enjoy the pleasure of sliding down a rainbow.

The following tips will help you maintain your joy and initiate a self-care attitude when you are facing challenges, mastering your goals and manifesting dreams. They will facilitate the EmPowerShifted life!

Prioritize your life to find balance.

"I've learned that you can't have everything and do everything at the same time."
— Oprah Winfrey

Know what is important in your life and in what order it is ranked. It does no good to manifest your dreams and master your goals and lose your health in the process. You determine your goals and manage your challenges; do not allow your goals or challenges to determine and manage your life.

Get adequate amounts of sleep

"It is useless for you to work so hard from early morning until late at night, anxiously working for food to eat; for God gives rest to his loved ones."
— Psalm 127:2 (NLT)

We need sleep to survive and thrive. However, sleeping can become a struggle when we worry about problems and focus on what tomorrow may bring. Or, a good night's sleep may be denied to watch late-night television, text messages on the cell phone, send e-mail on the computer or engage in other diversions of hi-tech life. We inappropriately think that we can manipulate our sleep regulator without any consequences. Experts believe that lack of sleep can cause mental and physical health problems as well as increase the risk of accidents and injury. At the very least, we throw the body's internal clock out of sync and find ourselves working harder and accomplishing less.

Get proper nutrition and stay hydrated.

"The wise man should consider that health is the greatest of human blessings. Let food be your medicine."
— *Hippocrates*

Proper nutrition supports life. A poor diet can have an adverse effect on both physical and mental health. Establishing healthy eating patterns can have a positive effect on the body and mind. Find a diet that is balanced for you and includes all the nutrients your body needs to function properly. Junk food may stop the hunger pangs and cravings but it is low in nutritional value and high in salts, fats, sugar and calories. Remember to drink water! Maintaining hydration is a key to good physical and mental performance.

Remember to breathe!

"Breathe. Let go. And remind yourself that this very moment is the only one you know you have for sure."
— *Oprah Winfrey*

Breathing delivers oxygen where it is needed and also removes waste. Your breath drives the nervous system and provides the majority of your energy. When we are stressed, our breathing may not stay in balance and our reactions to stressors can become distorted or magnified. This can create further anxiety. Failing to breathe properly also tightens and restricts your body. The energy flow inhibited by shallow breathing may therefore continue to trigger more physiological or psychological responses. Breathing naturally allows us to address our stressors in a more rational manner. As we change our breathing, we can change the state of our body and mind. Discover meditation and prayer practices that focus on breath work to induce a state of quietness of mind and body.

Address your stress!

"There is more to life than increasing its speed."
Mahatma Gandhi

When joy and peace are replaced by stress, your body can ache and your head can pound from tension. Physical manifestations of stress need to be addressed. Slow down. Roll your shoulders, stretch, breathe and go for a walk. Take a few minutes away from your stressor and recharge your body and brain.

Plan for R &R (rest and relaxation) in your day planner, PDA or wall calendar.

"If bread is the first necessity of life, recreation is a close second."
— Edward Bellamy

Make an appointment with yourself, and just yourself, for two hours a week. Take time out to go see a movie. Go for a walk in the park or a stroll on a beach. Plan a bubble-bath with candles and music or attend the opening of an art gallery. Get a massage. Turn off the telephones, computers and television. Do not answer calls or check e-mails. Plan time to recharge.

Give yourself permission to have fun and to laugh!

"Laughter is an instant vacation."
— *Milton Berle*

Laughter and fun are two of the greatest stress relievers. You do not have to be under stress to master your goals and be considered a success. Past studies indicated that people used to laugh an average of 18 minutes a day. Today, the time frame for laughter has been reduced to approximately six minutes. When I was competing in horse shows, my coach always reminded me, "If you aren't having fun, you shouldn't be out there." Don't take yourself so seriously all the time! Have fun and laugh!

Celebrate your success and your significance!

To laugh often and much; to win the respect of intelligent people and the affection of children...to leave the world a better place...to know even one life has breathed easier because you have lived. This is to have succeeded." Ralph Waldo Emerson

Take time to honor your achievements. In the effort to achieve goals, many times we overlook so much of what we have already accomplished. When we are faced with challenges, we fail to give ourselves the credit due for dealing with that which we are experiencing. Take a "Wow!" moment. Slow down to celebrate and appreciate your achievements. Give significance to your successes.

In the quest for success, we may fail to see that we are already living much of that life that we have envisioned for ourselves. I have experienced personal moments of self-doubt about the significance of my life. A friend once asked me what it was that I saw myself doing professionally. The competitive side of my nature wanted to prove to the outer world that I could work in a law firm, make partner and enjoy all of the trappings that come with the title. This, for a fleeting moment might have made me feel successful; however, it definitely would not have made me feel significant.

What did I see for my professional life? I envisioned myself working with a select group of clients, assisting them in transitions and transformation and affecting their lives in a positive manner. At the same time, I desired to work in a peaceful supportive environment.

I hesitated for a moment as the enlightenment became clear. I realized that I had already achieved the measure of "success" I described. This level of success was not as grand as my vision, but it was manifesting in my daily life. I was working from a home office where I could look out my window and watch my horses peacefully graze in the pasture. At the same time, I was completing my projects, papers and other "at work" tasks. Office coffee breaks and water cooler chats were substituted with quiet moments during the day to walk out to the barn.

My client base was largely referrals from past clients and friends. I had traded my stressful morning commute in traffic for a morning meditation and exercise routine. I was teaching teenagers and adults how to ride and communicate with horses in the afternoon, sharing a gift that I had been given by a mentor. Perhaps by society's success standard it wasn't grand and glorious; however, it was significant to me. I was facilitating positive changes in people's lives and living my purpose. Remember, just because the instrument is not one that we expect to play, doesn't mean that the music is any less beautiful.

There is a tendency to measure our goals and dreams against success as defined by those around us. In doing so, ego may get in the way. Many times, the physical world quantifies success by measuring elements such as power, wealth and material possessions. At the same time, society may equate success with the number of dollars in a money market account, the tangible material possessions one owns or the number of times one has been promoted in the community or workplace. Importance may be placed on what people have rather than who they are.

This model can prove to be a downward spiral. The effort to be successful solely by material standards may create unhappiness, fear, bitterness and resentment as a by-product. If the amount of money you have determines your success, why are there people who are rich and unhappy? If influence and status define success, why are there people who have attained power and remain possessed by fear and uncertainty? The ego judges success by the external standards. The soul goes within and seeks knowledge, understanding and significance. Success without significance is empty. Significance evolves from living a life in purpose, mastering your goals and manifesting your dreams.

> *PowerShift Reflection – I am already successful and significant. My unique greatness is within me. I choose to live the EmPowerShifted Life and dance to the music that is within my own soul!*

"In moments where I actually had the time to think about what was going on in my life, I contemplated the number and severity of the challenges that I had experienced. Had I signed some unknown karmic contract? Was I atoning for actions in a past life? Could all of this be just some fortuitous roll of the dice? Or, had I done something to irritate or disappoint God? The answers to my questions became clearer as I navigated each challenge. "

— *Tamara Vaughn*

The answers became clear. I am leading an EmPowerShifted life. My life has always been blessed, especially through the challenge and adversities I have overcome. When I take a moment and reflect on the events that seemingly tore my world apart and rocked my foundation, I can see that there were always the unseen blessings buried beneath the tragedy. The

PowerShifts gave me the power to persevere and make my goals and dreams my reality through my life's purpose.

What have I learned through my challenges and adversities? What lessons empower me to live a life in purpose, master my goals and manifest my dreams?

I have learned that:

- My greatest growth and self-development have developed from living my greatest challenges.

- Challenges and adversity have charted my path to my purpose and have allowed me to discover talents, gifts and resources to master my goals and manifest my dreams.

- Through my challenges and adversity, I have developed the unique ability to help others who face similar challenges.

- Challenges and adversity have clarified my beliefs and values and remind me of what is important in my life.

- There is not enough time in the day for me to list all that I have in my life for which I am grateful.

And, I have learned that there is a Divine plan of goodness and greatness for my life.

Your dreams come from God and God will help you accomplish them. In this Divine order there may be challenges and adversity on the path to your goals and dreams. Sometimes pain, or a level of discomfort, is what it takes to make us discover gifts, talents and blessings that we have abandoned or overlooked.

"To give less than your best is to sacrifice the gift."
— Steve Prefontaine

Adversity can bring out the best in us and inspire us to acknowledge our significance. Challenges can lead us to deliver our gift and our greatness to the world in our own unique way.   When the soul embraces adversity, rather than resisting it, the challenge becomes a catalyst for growth, inspiration and motivation.

"Life's challenges are not supposed to paralyze you,
they're supposed to help you discover who you are."
— Bernice Johnson Reagon

I invite you to:
Empower yourself with the knowledge that the
only power a person, situation, challenge or adversity has
in your life is the power you choose to give it.

Empower yourself with the knowledge that the power your
Purpose, Goals and Dreams have is the power that you choose to give
them.Embrace the EmPowerShifted life!

Live your life in Purpose,
Master your GOALS, and
Manifest your DREAMS!
Shift the Power!

This page provided for your personal PowerShift notes, reflections, and thoughts.